Praise for Gold Vision

"Hisano-san challenges us to look beyond what is familiar and what is comfortable. To seek the sub-conscious you by leaving the circle of familiarity and to seek interaction with those that will enable you to grow. Gold Vision is as much about mastering self-help as it is about a focused coaching approach to achieve that which you truly wish to achieve. From Japanese philosophy to western application Hisano-san and his Gold Vision approach will help you find you the way to transcend and break through your status quo and achieve your unachievable. If you want to change the direction you are headed in and be the 'who' you want to be then I highly recommend the Gold Vision approach."

> – Nigel Thurlow, former Chief of Agile at Toyota, co-author/creator of *The Flow System,* recognized expert consultant and speaker on Lean, Agile, Complexity Thinking, Leadership and Team Science.

Gold Vision is a must read if you want to make your life's dreams come true. Kazuyosi Hisano debunks misguided paths to a good life and masterfully assembles everything you need to create a fulfilling and happy life.

> – John M. Bernard, Author of the best-selling *Business at the Speed of Now* and *Government That Works*

"As Mr. Hisano stated in this book, we need an absolute standard for moving toward a global level. Unlike most people who are just satisfied with living with dreams and ideals, it tells us that we can create new things that no one has ever thought of by having a grand vision that goes beyond the present situation and limits. This book gives us valuable wisdom to have Gold Vision, a force that transcends the present state and creates a dynamic new future for us who are the leaders of this era."

> – David Dongchul Bae, founder of Asia Future HR Institute, CEO at Startup Forum in Korea, leading businessman and strategist selected as "100 CEOs to Lead Asia for the Next Generation" by The Japan Times

---

"Most of us look at life like a passenger looking out of the rear windscreen of a car. We constantly analyze the past and even when we imagine the future, it is a projection based on past experiences.

Sensei Hisano shows us how to take the driver's seat. He gives us a toolkit to clarify our goals, align them to our innermost values and make them a reality.

Using principles of cognitive science and real life examples, this book is a step-by-step guide. Whether you are a chief executive or someone at the start of your career, this book can be an asset to your professional and personal life."

> – Suresh T.V., President, Tao Consulting Systems

"The late Norman Bodek, my dear friend and mentor, introduced me to Mr. Kazuyoshi Hisano's work on Gold Vision and I am forever grateful for it. Norman earned his nickname, Godfather of Lean, for his visionary work bringing the concept to the West in early 1980s. He used to say that he had a gift of attracting the world's greatest geniuses and wisdom. Kazuyoshi Hisano became the last person in Norman's long chain of luminaries.

Gold Vision is a groundbreaking book that offers practical insights into the world of neuroscience and the power of the subconscious mind. Through thought-provoking examples and case studies, the author shows readers how to harness the immense potential of the subconscious to achieve their goals and unlock their true potential. This book is a must-read for anyone looking to tap into the limitless power of their subconscious and take control of their lives."

> – Ahmed Avais, Business Agility Coach, CEO of Agile 7, Coach of agile coaches and scrum masters

---

"I had the blessing of being introduced to Norman Bodek, then president of PCS Press, in 2018. I was immediately amazed by his energy and passion to make a positive impact on the world. He loved coaching people, teaching Lean and all the best practices he had experienced in Japan and connecting great minds together. We spent time together reflecting on how to make Leaders more socially responsible—that was an important topic for him and the subject of his last book *The Leader's Guide for Social Responsibility*.

One core aspect of Leadership is the capability to define a great long-term vision and to achieve it by developing people and bringing the best out of them. Norman himself was a passionate coach and he learned advanced aspects of coaching and change management with Kazuyoshi Hisano, which he considered "the world's greatest coach". He taught me the details of Hisano-san's approach during multiple zoom calls. I had the chance to have a one on one coaching session with Hisaso-san in 2020 and tried out the method for my teams and for me. Until now I am still applying the core aspects of it to stay focused on my own goals and to develop my managers into future leaders. Using cognitive psychology and daily routines really helped me develop myself and achieve goals which otherwise I am not sure I would have achieved. I really recommend the book *Gold Vision* for those reasons, and I am grateful to Hisano-san for his great pieces of advice."

– Christophe Makni, Lean Leader and Executive at a Financial Institution

---

"Want a better career? Want more money? Want a new house? Want [you name it]? Look no further. Back in May 2020 I had the privilege to be coached by the late Norman Bodek, who was known as the "godfather of lean." At that time, Norman introduced me to the teachings of the "Best Coach of the World," as he used to refer to Mr. Kazuyoshi Hisano, the author of the book you are now holding. Mr. Hisano presents a compelling case on how to use your brain to finally achieve your goals and get out of your comfort zone. This could be the end of the self-help books"

– Alberto Molinar, CEO, Global Audit

"You don't need to be the CEO of a multi-billion company or a top athlete to use Gold Vision. Mr. Hisano takes your hand and shows you how to excel in any aspect of your life, be it family, career or health. This is a truly life changing book. I know because it changed mine. "

– Nihat Karaoglu, Tech Executive, Switzerland

GOLD VISION

GOLD
VISION

See Your Future

Believe In Yourself

Involve And Move People

KAZUYOSHI HISANO

PCS PRESS

Seattle, Washington

Publisher's Cataloging-in-Publication data

Names: Hisano, Kazuyoshi, author.

Title: Gold vision : see your future , believe in yourself , involve and move people / Kazuyoshi Hisano.

Description: Includes bibliographical references and index. | Seattle, WA: PCS Press, 2023.

Identifiers: LCCN: 2022951651 | ISBN: 979-8-9872585-0-7 (paperback) | 979-8-9872585-1-4 (Kindle)

Subjects: LCSH Success--Psychological aspects. | Goal (Psychology) | Self-actualization (Psychology) | Self-help. | BISAC SELF-HELP / Personal Growth / Success | SELF-HELP / Self-Management / General | SELF-HELP / Motivational & Inspirational.

Classification: LCC BF637.S8 .H57 2023 | DDC 650.1--dd23

PCS Press

PCS Inc.

1420 5TH AVE, STE 4200

SEATTLE, WA 98101-2375

1-360-605-7508

Printed in the United States of America

Edited by Bob Quinn and Beth Simone, and translated by Noriko Hosoyamada. The cover and book design is by Bobbi Benson, Wild Ginger Press.

*To my wife Seiko Hisano
and my son Sho Hisano.*

CONTENTS

FOREWORD

After receiving a number of coaching sessions from *Gold Visions's* author Kazuyoshi Hisano, the late Norman Bodek, former president of PCS Inc. and my husband, articulated his personal vision as follows: "My goal is to continue to discover the world's greatest management wisdom to help people live better lives. I want to help leaders to develop themselves to manage socially responsible organizations. I want people to love coming to work and make their companies a great place to be."

This note to himself was dated 11/25/2020, a couple weeks before his sudden departure from this world at the age of 88. He certainly lived his life fully until the very end and had finished his project of producing *CEO Coaching* by Kazuyoshi Hisano. In line with his goal, Norman was planning next to start the project of translating and publishing *Gold Vision* from Japanese into English. In his spirit, we at PCS decided to carry this project forward. Though it took much longer than we hoped for, we are happy to make it available for readers in this form.

Lately, I often hear Mr. Hisano saying, "What you need to achieve the results you want in life boils down to really two things—to dream up your future and to act on it." In this book he covers both aspects quite extensively.

While the Prologue, Introduction, Closing, and Epilogue of this book provide for readers the framework and background of how and why Mr. Hisano developed his Gold Vision Method, each chapter gives you specific methodologies you can apply for envisioning your own shining future with Gold Vision and making it happen. The book includes the rich experiences of Mr. Hisano personally applying what he learned on this subject for decades, as well as with many of his coaching clients.

In Chapter 1, the author starts with a provocative question: Why is it that the more you think about wanting something, the less likely you are to get it, while a relatively small number of people seem to be able to get what they want. Referring to cognitive science findings, Mr. Hisano explains that it depends on an individual's perception of himself/herself as a resident of the world having or not having something. He goes on to explain our brain's tendency to maintain the status quo, as well as the function of the RAS (Reticular Activating System), that selectively takes in the information that the brain perceives as important.

In Chapter 2, Mr. Hisano emphasizes the importance of setting a high goal, well outside of our current status quo and which represents what our heart really wants. Then, we need to enhance the sense of reality in the desired new status quo by making our subconscious our ally.

In Chapter 3, the author encourages us to envision our goals on three axes: greatness, wanting to, and many. He underscores the importance of "many" to make our whole life happy. This chapter introduces the Balance Wheel, a tool to help develop our goals in multiple aspects of our life. Then, he touches upon three powers necessary to materialize our Gold Vision, which are explained in depth in the chapters that follow.

Chapter 4 introduces the first power: "The power to see the future," one of the three powers required for materializing our Gold Vision. Mr. Hisano challenges us to think about the prevailing notion of time flowing from the past to the present and to the future. He presents the perspective that time flows from the future to the present and to the past.

Chapter 5 introduces the second power: "The power to believe in yourself." Our self-efficacy is a product of our thought habits, especially at the subconscious level. He encourages us to first become aware of our "bubble-up" type self-talks and replace them with "imprint" type. In this process we create new circuits in the brain favorable for our Gold Vision.

Chapter 6 introduces the third power: "The power to involve and move people." In this chapter, Mr. Hisano elaborates the aspect of acting on our Gold Vision. He talks about how to become a resident of your goal world, leaving behind the current status quo. He offers us specific strategies to develop and cultivate supporting human relations necessary for achieving Gold Vision.

"I'm finally behind the steering wheel of my life. I mean I now feel I can go in any direction I want to." This is what one of Mr. Hisano's clients said when he found his own Gold Vision. We will be more than happy if this book can contribute to readers finding their Gold Vision for a happier life.

Noriko Hosoyamada
Publisher

PROLOGUE

Let's assume there are two people who have different perspectives and habits.

Person A:

With her ambition to be an international businessperson, she has been studying hard during her school days and has been working hard as an adult.

Aiming for further advancement, she is living her life enthusiastically every day, while always **stretching herself personally and professionally as much as possible, and setting goals slightly ahead of what is reachable for her.**

Person B:

This person is always exploring things that he finds interesting at the moment; he is always talking about crazy dreams, most of them unrealistic.

People around him advise him, "You'd better focus more on reality."

Both Person A and Person B are still young now, and assume their lives will be filled with success, both financially and in other ways.

The Key Question:

At the last moment of life, which of the two people, Person A or Person B, would likely utter the words,

"Ah, it was such a happy life!"?

The answer is Person B.

Unexpected?

In fact, the latest cognitive science has revealed that **"Setting a wrong goal** surprisingly **prevents us from growing."**

What is a "wrong" goal?

What mistake did Person A make?

In this book, we will explore many common beliefs and show why they should be thrown out.

We ask you to read this book with an open mind and be prepared to enter **the world of breakthroughs with Gold Vision.**

INTRODUCTION

What is Gold Vision?

A Robust Approach About How to
Change Yourself and Achieve Your Goals

Thank you for picking up this book. My name is Kazuyoshi Hisano, a professional coach.

You may be like so many people and feel that you are busy every day, and your life seems to be more or less satisfactory on the surface. However, you might be noticing a somewhat uneasy feeling about yourself deep down. If you do notice this uneasy feeling, you might not know specifically what it is and what you should do about it.

If you are in a hazy, dull state of mind—as many people are these days—it might be difficult for you to stir up much energy and enthusiasm for achieving the best results at work, even though the desire might be strong inside you.

As a professional coach, my job is to help as many people as possible become aware of their innate capabilities and how they can maximize them. Through meeting a large number of my clients on a daily basis, what I observe is that many people are feeling anxious and dissatisfied with their current situation and are asking themselves, "Is it alright for me to stay where I am at currently, or should I make a change?"

This feeling seems to be the same even if from the outside their job and company might be one others admire and they may receive a high income. The biggest problem is that many people do not know what their true goals are.

If you find yourself in a situation like this, do not worry. There is a method that you can use to change things within yourself to help you achieve your goals and move up to a new state of greater fulfillment and happiness. That's what my Gold Vision Method does for people.

The Gold Vision Method is the program that I developed based on my many years working as a corporate and personal coach. I want to be clear the Gold Vision Method is not a loose system based simply on anecdotes from my clients. The basis of this method is the discipline based on well-developed cognitive science, which has evolved considerably in recent decades, as artificial intelligence has developed. Cognitive science is closely related to other disciplines, such as computational linguistics, cognitive psychology, and analytical philosophy. It is greatly influ-encing the paradigms of many branches of science.

Needless to say, cognitive science is an actual science. Therefore, the results that it brings about are not fuzzy. This is a major difference between science and simple ideas or experiences.

As the Gold Vision Method is based on cognitive science, you can expect to produce the desired results when you follow the methodology. In fact, many clients of mine have materialized amazing results through the Gold Vision Method. From the theoretical viewpoints of cognitive science, such achievements are totally natural and to be expected.

Moreover, when you make your brain an ally, you don't have to work nearly so hard. You will become able to achieve all kinds of things naturally. You may be wondering, "Is such a thing really possible?" By learning how to use your brain as cognitive science reveals, however, anyone can achieve his/her hoped for results.

Support for Effectively Using the Brain and the Mind

Before getting into the main topics of this book, let me briefly explain what coaching is. All human thought and action are derived from the brain and mind. The coach's job is to help people make good use of them.

It is said that the term "coach" was born in the area currently known as Hungary in the 15th century. Initially, it meant "carriage," but it was broadened to mean "means to move people to their destinations." These days, it also refers to types of transportation, such as buses and airplanes.

So, a coach is a person whose role is to support others getting to their destinations. The coach's role is to help someone achieve his/her goals. Therefore, the necessary premise for coaching is that the coachee have a goal. If the person working with the coach does not have a clearly articulated goal, then the process begins with the coach helping them to identify it. You must first know where you want to go before you can start your journey.

From sports to businesses, presently there are many people who are called "coaches." Coaching in sports is popular of course. Generally speaking, the role of a typical sport coach heavily emphasizes the teaching of technical skills. Therefore, it could be said that their role may be rather closer to an "instructor" than a "coach."

On the other hand, coaches in the business world are often confused with "consultants." A consultant's job is to teach how to *solve* specific problems. This works well in many cases. A coach's job, however, is to teach how to *find* the solutions to the problems. In another word, consultants give the results of "the fish" to the client, whereas coaches give the client a fishing pole and teach them how to fish, as well as how to come up with a better fishing method. The point is not which is better. Each has its own characteristics. The primary merit of coaching is its "adaptability" to help each individual person.

A mentor plays a similar role as a coach. A mentor often means "guide" or "advisor." In many cases, a mentor refers to a person with higher seniority at the workplace playing the role of helping others think and make decisions. Relatively speaking, a mentor tends to offer mental support and the mentor's relationship to the mentee tends to be looser than that of a coach, whose purpose is to take the coachee to their desired destination.

Coaching for the Japanese to Achieve Better Results

It has been more than 15 years since the coaching theory that Lou Tice, a well-regarded American coach, created first came to Japan. Lou Tice is who I learned coaching from and the Gold Vision Method is built on what I learned from him.

Presently in Japan, the concept of coaching is quite diverse. The popularization of coaching in Japan has to be recognized as a helpful trend.

Intrinsically, coaching is not a simple technique for questioning and communicating; rather it is an approach that can enhance human capabilities in all directions.

I use the term "all directions" meaning that coaching can enhance the satisfaction level of all aspects of one's life, not only in the career arena but also in family relationships, in relationships with friends, in our pursuit of our hobbies, in our health, and in our broad social contributions. Those who are interested I encourage you to read Lou Tice's books.

Originally, Lou Tice developed his coaching theory based on psychology, establishing the program of his coaching method. His program is widely recognized in the United States and has been introduced to many organizations, including the Department of Defense, NASA, federal government agencies, and more than the half of the Fortune 500 companies. It can be said that his theory played an important role at the core of the US business development at that time.

Since then, his theory has been disseminated to foreign governmental organizations and companies, as well as those who are the heads of a state and CEOs in world enterprises. Thus, the concept has become highly respected around the world.

Michael Phelps, the swimmer who won 23 Olympic gold medals (as of 2016 Rio Olympics) in swimming, a world record, has learned Lou Tice's method from Mark Schubert, the legendary swimming coach, who used to be one of the 8 U.S. Olympic Team staff members. Mark and Lou had been good friends for a long time until Lou Tice passed away in 2012. Mark Shubert is one of my mentors whom I meet once every few years.

Lou Tice made remarkable achievements in other sports as well, sometimes supporting teams by himself and sometimes through his students. I know many coaches who directly and indirectly learned his method. He played a significant role in popularizing the concept of coaching.

However, Lou Tice did not rest on his laurels. Originally, he was a coach for a high-school football team and had a vision to teach coaching to young people around the world. In this vein, he adopted the paradigm of cognitive science, which was further advancing psychology. At this time, Hideto

Tomobechi, Ph.D, a world-renowned cognitive scientist, was the one who brought the cutting-edge findings of cognitive science to Lou Tice. After Lou Tice passed away, Dr. Tomabechi became one of his successors and spread this coaching message, not only in Japan, but all over the world. He worked to further develop Lou Tice's coaching theory.

Later, I will talk more about how my coaching method has developed in detail but let me touch on my own brief history. Prior to starting my current work, my experiences included starting a business as an entrepreneur and working at multiple multinational corporations.

In order to achieve good results in my work, I took many seminars and read loads of books on self-development in search of hints for growing myself. When I encountered Dr. Tomabechi's book, I felt that finally this was what I was searching for. As I applied his coaching method at work, I was excited to see the results I was achieving.

Consequently, I had an opportunity to meet Dr. Tomabechi in person and started to learn from him to the point that I myself became active in coaching after being certified as a professional coach. As a coach, I started to achieve excellent results with my clients.

I believe that this was because I fully applied the knowledge and skills I learned from Mr. Lou Tice and Dr. Tomabechi. On the other hand, I have accumulated over time my experiences and gradually added what I thought and learned to improve the concept. At one point I felt that I had developed something new on the "shoulders of these giants" and I decided to launch my Gold Vision Method. While I respect both masters, I wanted and needed to create something that fits the contemporary era. I incorporated my own experiences as an executive and a businessperson as well as added some new arrangements and further developed the existing method.

So far, I have worked with thousands of people, including top executives of many organizations, professionals of all sorts, including medical doctors, lawyers, accountants, and businesspersons and salespersons in many different fields. I also coach top athletes of various sports. Coaching them with the Gold Vision Method individually or in a group has brought positive changes to so many lives.

As for organizational coaching, many common issues are brought to me for consultations from management. These issues include "vitalization of an organization," "uplifting motivation," "creation of innovation," "new business start-up," and "enhancing the sales force." Among these, the most important issue for executives and managers is how to generate innovation. I am often asked to teach how to bring about innovations utilizing the Gold Vision Method.

It is possible to gain a different vantage point on your field, higher than before by using the Gold Vision Method. It means that you will be able to notice what others are yet to recognize and to apply your findings to your business. Thus, the Gold Vision Method can effectively help you create innovations and launch new businesses.

There are many examples. One of them is a company with computer graphics capabilities that has provided their services to the customers in the construction industry. Then the recession caused by the spread of COVID-19 in 2020 hit them harshly resulting in a great loss in sales. Subsequently, they applied the Gold Vision Method and established their brand-new products of VR (Virtual Reality) and AR (Augmented Reality) by capitalizing on their capabilities to create beautiful computer graphics.

The other example is about the salespersons in the life insurance industry, a few of whom I personally coached. Two of them have been the Japanese champions in their respective companies (each of the companies has 4000 and 9000 salespersons) for the past three years in a row. They are expected to continue their journey in the future as they are so dominant in their field. They are always creative in finding new approaches to promote and sell their products.

The Gold Vision method has helped and is helping them come up with brand-new ideas.

While the issues that companies and executives face might be diverse, such as "innovation," "launching new businesses," and "enhancing the sales force," it is possible to achieve greater results by utilizing the common framework of my Gold Vision Method. Whether individuals or organizations make use of the Gold Vision Method, many cases prove its effectiveness in achieving the desired results.

Gold Vision is Something You Create

Gold Vision is a term that I came up with meaning "GOLD (of great value)" and "GOALED (a goal that has been already materialized.)" I don't think "GOALED" is a proper English term, but I coined the word to convey the nuance of "already materialized."

When you can feel your bright future as if it has already happened, I strongly believe that you can achieve anything. Gold Vision is the future that you yourself can create.

How, then, can we set our own Gold Vision, our self-created future? How can we materialize it? I intend to answer these questions and discuss the method in this book. In short, the following three powers are the keys:

- The power to see the future.
- The power to believe in yourself.
- The power to involve and move people.

It is my sincere hope that the readers of this book will make use of it for acquiring these three powers, drawing out his/her maximum potential, and flourishing in his/her life. If this book helps the readers find their own true goals and achieve them, there is no greater joy for me.

Summary
- Gold Vision is the bright, sparkling future that you feel as if it has already happened.
- To materialize the above, you need three powers: "the power to see the future," "the power to believe in yourself" and "the power to involve and move people."

CHAPTER 1

What Prevents Many People From Achieving Their Goals?

The More You Think About Wanting Something, the Less Likely You Are to Get It

Have you ever experienced any of the following? The more you want to earn, the more you seem to be blocked from your goal. The more you want to sell, the more difficult it is for you to reach your sales goal. The more you want to lose weight, the more you seem to be stymied from reaching your target weight. The more you want to be popular with certain new love interests, the more this goal seems elusive. We can probably go on and on adding to this list of examples. Why are we so unlikely to get what we want, the more we desire it?

Going straight to the point, those who want something are often stuck living in a world of lacking it. For example, those who want to earn more are often living in the world where not earning enough is their actual reality. Therefore, they end up staying in the state of being unable to earn more. This lack is what dominates their awareness.

On the other side of this apparent mystery, there are a relatively small number of people who can effectively earn what they want or even more. They are residents in the world of earning well, not in a world of *not* achieving their goals. The performance of an individual does not really depend on what s/he is hoping for; rather it depends on which world s/he lives in.

How do we become residents in the world of not earning enough? It is actually related to what is going on in our brains.

The major premise is this: The brain cannot recognize and maintain two worlds at the same time. Figure 1-1 is a famous drawing.

If you focus on the white, it looks like a goblet. If you focus on the black, you see the profile of two people. However, it is impossible to see both at the same time. Some may say, "I can see both simultaneously," but they are merely switching back and forth very rapidly. This is strongly related to what I am going to explain about how the brain works.

Figure 1-1: What do you see?

The world we see is the aggregate of what our brain considers important. In the brainstem at the base of the brain, there exists the "Reticular Activating System (RAS)" that functions as a filter for the information coming in from the outside environment. We notice only the things that the RAS has filtered in and identified as "important."

As mentioned before, the brain cannot recognize and maintain two pieces of information at the same time. Thus, we tend to miss the things that the brain considers not important.

Let's look now at the Figure 1-2. How many triangles do you see?

If your answer is one, two, three, etc., it is incorrect. The correct answer is zero. There are no triangles at all in this

Figure 1-2: How many triangles do you see?

picture because a triangle is defined as a three-sided polygon. It consists of three points in a plane connected by three straight lines. In this picture, there is nothing that meets this definition.

Nevertheless, we look in the picture for triangles that do not exist. It is due to the conditioning in our brain given by the question, "How many triangles do you see?"

What if you were simply looking at the same picture, without having been asked about triangles? You would probably see some straight lines and black circles with a missing part.

Like this example, when important things (in this case triangles) are determined through conditioning, the RAS prevents us from seeing things that are unimportant. Thus, in the shapes which are not triangles at all, we see triangles viewed from our conditioned mind.

Let's go back to the example of wanting to earn more. If we probe into the mind of a person who is wanting to earn more, s/he has the desire to do so, because s/he is not earning as much as hoped for. Thus, it is probable that s/he lives in the world of not-earning.

If this is the case, can we predict what will happen? If you live in the world of not-earning as much as you want to, and you think about it over and over, your brain becomes impregnated with a strong message that you are not earning at your desired level. Thus, you end up conditioning yourself in the reverse direction of what you hope to achieve. As a result, your RAS recognizes the state of not-earning as important, and you will end up only seeing the world of not-earning. It's extremely problematic, isn't it?

Then, what should we do if we are stuck in this dilemma?

Have no fear. The theme of this book is how you can solve this troublesome condition. The answers will be discussed in depth later in this book, but here let me explain another reason why the more you think about wanting something, the less likely you are to achieve it.

The Brain Loves Maintaining the Status Quo

When the RAS recognizes the state of not-earning (or not-selling) as important, it automatically tries to maintain it.

This is another reason why the more you think about a particular goal, the less likely you are to achieve it. The brain loves maintaining the status quo. It can be accurately described as an animal instinct for survival.

Cows in the field eat only grass and do not eat the mushrooms right next to the grass. It is because the cows' brains recognize only grass, which is important for their survival. They do not see other things that could possibly be eaten, including mushrooms. Eating grass in the meadow is what we call "the comfort zone" for cows.

The comfort zone refers to the state or space in which a person feels comfort—often because of familiarity. Interestingly, "comfort" for the brain that loves the status quo is different from our common notion of "comfort" in an ordinary sense.

For example, if we compare commuting in a crowded commuter train to being driven by a chauffeur in a limousine, we will generally feel more comfortable in the latter. However, for the brain of the people who commute daily in the crowded train, the crowded train represents a sort of comfort zone, because "comfort" for the brain is a familiar space to which we have accustomed ourselves.

Once the brain perceives the crowded train "comfort" and makes it into a "comfort zone," as we are defining it here, it is rather difficult to switch to the lifestyle of having a chauffeur-driven limousine. Please remember this term "comfort zone" as it appears often in the book and how we are defining it.

In the same way, the world of not-earning in the earlier example can become our "comfort zone."

Cows do not go out of their way to eat mushrooms by changing their comfort zone. The cows' brains seek to maintain the status quo by eating grass for their survival. It is exactly the right answer for the cows.

A human is an animal too. Instinctively, the human brain tries to maintain the status quo if it is left to its own devices. The more you want to do something, for example, making more money, the brain recognizes the status quo as being the state of not making more money. As this situation of not earning what we want to earn becomes the comfort zone, the brain tends to be further reinforced to maintain this status quo.

The Scotoma Called the Precedent

Over a long history, a cow's brain must have been continuously inputting the information that "Eating grass is staying alive." For cows eating grass can be said to be the actualization of this past information and habit. In the human world, we can call this having precedent.

As cows do not see the mushrooms next to the grass that they eat, the precedent ends up being a huge scotoma. Scotoma is the term often used in coaching; it is an area of diminished vision in the visual field. When we let nature take its course, the human brain, too, recognizes the important information from the past (the precedent) through the RAS and does not see the rest.

In another words, *we are living in a world made up of our memories from the past*. We are naturally that way. If we become slaves to precedents, our brain will reinforce more and more the status quo. This will make it difficult to break through the current situation, as we seek to create a new reality for ourselves.

Here, let us think about an example in Japan. It may differ from one country to another country, but generally speaking people in Japan tend to prefer "brand-new" things. This trend is apparent in signs such as "brand-new car" for cars, "brand-new construction" for houses, and "brand-new item" for clothes emphasizing "never been used before."

Under these preferences and tendencies, not many Japanese consider buying and using second-hand goods as their first choice. Unless there is a reason, such as a new item being too expensive, many try to choose a thing as new as possible.

Furthermore, even when they decide to buy a used car, they try to choose the one with the least mileage possible. Manufacturing companies also make products to suit such Japanese tastes.

This tendency is very different, I believe, from people in countries where they have a habit of using things a long time and carefully repairing them. Undeniably, the Japanese people's experiences living in a rare earthquake-prone country, where so many earthquakes have hit and instantly destroyed so many things, including houses, have contributed to forming such tendency.

In any case, Japanese people don't seem to have much sense that the value of the goods will increase by taking good care of, repairing them when damaged, and using them for a long time.

This is an example where the notion of "new things are more valuable than old ones" results in building a scotoma (blind spot) and not seeing the value of used items.

I often wonder why people in Japan are so concerned about newness for their personal belongings, despite the culture where many old things such as historic buildings are carefully maintained.

Meanwhile, this situation has started to change in recent years. It is due to the rapidly growing awareness in the world for protecting the global environment.

The term SDGs (Sustainable Development Goals) has become popular in Japan as well and begun changing people's consciousness. An emerging momentum is "let's use things carefully without being too particular about new things."

Nevertheless, the emphasis on getting "new things" has resulted in forming a scotoma in which the value of old things was not seen. People's consciousness has begun to change due to the external triggers called SDGs. In this way, we see that external influences can alter scotomas.

These changes, however, are still limited. Although small changes are beginning to occur, there still exists a strong tendency to seek new things in the main, and because the society and companies are designed in that way, sweeping changes are challenging to institute. Thus, the prevailing status quo will be maintained and continued.

A battle always remains between the new trend and the status quo for a long time. We may relate to the transformation of gender equality and overall diversity in the society as another example.

Many of you might have had some experiences in which new ideas were not accepted because of a given precedent. From the viewpoint of the way the brain works, organizations do not allow for an experience outside of precedents. Such a company will inevitably be unable to stay current with the times and will be destined to decline.

This principle applies to individuals as well as organizations. If we do nothing, our instinct is set to maintain the status quo. Thus, if we continue inputting the information that was important in the past, we will not be able to move forward.

Animal Goals vs Human Goals

There is a big difference between animals and humans. The goal of animals is to maintain the status quo dictated by their survival instinct. On the other hand, the goal of humans is not just for survival. The reason why humans have been able to build great civilizations is because humans were not satisfied with the status quo, and they repeatedly transformed it by setting higher goals.

Letters, numbers, clothing, many tools, printing, light bulbs, radios, automobile, television, drugs, computers, etc., all these things around us are the products of breakthroughs at the time. If humans had always been satisfied merely with the status quo, we would probably still be living like we did in the stone age.

These breakthroughs are what the Gold Vision of certain trail-blazing humans brought about. Since we are humans, we must be capable of progressing beyond the current situation. Moreover, we are at a point in time when change can occur at a bewildering speed. In this day and age, it would be difficult even to survive if we were always locked into the status quo.

Then, what should we, whose brains love the status quo, do to help these same brains work for us in materializing our respective Gold Visions? Starting in the next chapter, I will explain concrete methods you can employ that are based on the theories of cognitive science.

Summary

- The brain loves the status quo.
- If we do nothing, we are likely to maintain and fortify our familiar, current situation, rather than create the situation we wish to achieve.

CHAPTER 2

Transcend and Break Through the Status Quo With Gold Vision

World-Class Companies Have Gold Vision

In the previous chapter, I talked about past human civilizations having progressed with Gold Vision. The same is true in the present time. Walt Disney alone was able to see a clear vision of the Cinderella Castle on the cleared land in California when there was not yet a Disney Land. It was all still just a vision.

The other people around him, including his brother Roy, laughed it off as a mere fantasy. Nevertheless, together with his designer, Walt put this clear, detailed vision in his mind down on paper, talked to the potential investors passionately about it, and in the end managed to create the entire Magic Kingdom out of his imagination.

When Steve Jobs founded Apple, computers were limited to the use of the military and big corporations. He had the unique vision to create and provide personal computers to ordinary people, and he manifested it.

Then he publicly said, "We're here to put a dent in the universe" and motivated his employees to create products that no one had ever seen.

We see that with his extraordinary vision in the iPad, iPod, and iPhone, which completely changed the lives and cultures of people all over the world.

Google has long maintained its position as a world-leading brand; its stated vision is "to provide access to the world's information in one click." Presently we take it for granted, but I wonder how many people had envisioned the world we are now in before Google did.

I have seen these same types of companies in my own country of Japan.

Standing on a box for packing oranges, President Masayoshi Son of Softbank, declared he would create a business of $10 billions[1] in several decades when he started the company. At that time, it was so tiny that it could not be called even a small- or medium-sized company. It is said that the employees and part-timers at that time who heard him talk

---

1 In the original Japanese book, it is written "one trillion yen." For the sake of simplicity, the exchange rate of one dollar to 100 yen is used throughout the book.

of this large vision felt it was crazy and unrealistic and left the company. Of course, Softbank indeed eventually grew as Mr. Son had declared.

A long time before Mr. Son's time, there was a well-known episode in which Mr. Soichiro Honda, the founder of Honda Motor, also stood up on a packing crate and declared: "Honda will be a worldwide company!" Of course, we all know that he succeeded.

As you can see in these examples of famous and successful companies, it is impossible to create something new unless you have a high vision that transcends the current situation. It should be something that everyone else thinks is "impossible" or "unrealistic" and that nobody else has yet thought about and created.

That is the essence of what we call Gold Vision. The companies that grow to become world-class companies have such a vision that transcends the current situation and breaks through to create a dynamic new future; thus, they are able to truly prosper.

It's Actually Easier to Achieve a High Goal Than a Low Goal

Having read thus far, some of you might have felt that the reason why Walt Disney and Steve Jobs could make the impossible possible is because they were geniuses.

Indeed, they were geniuses, as they intuitively acquired Gold Vision.

However, there is no reason why we can't also be just

like them. Even if we may think we are not geniuses like them, it is not that difficult to find and achieve our own Gold Vision. What we need is to learn how our brain works. We need to discover the secret of the brain to break through the status quo and reach our goals.

What is needed, first and foremost, is to set a goal. When we set a goal, it starts to permeate into our subconscious mind and then the subconscious starts to work. Without setting a clear goal, the subconscious does not work for us to help us achieve our goal.

By the way, when you set a goal, it will work on your subconscious more powerfully if you write it down on a sheet of paper and read it aloud from time to time, rather than simply imagining it in your mind.

Furthermore, like Mr. Masayoshi Son, who declared his vision while standing on the box for packing oranges, it is important that your new vision be clearly outside of your current status quo.

If your annual income is $50,000, you might want to set the new goal at $500,000.

If your TOEIC[2] score is 400, you may want to set it at 950. (Among businesspeople in Japan, many try to challenge for this test. When they can get a score higher than 800 out of 990 as the highest and put it in their resume, it is beneficial for their prospects of changing their jobs or promotion within the company.)

"That's impossible," you may be saying. To transcend

2 TOEIC: The Test of English for International Communication is an international standardized test of English language proficiency for non-native speakers, with the highest possible score 990.

and break through the status quo, your goal must be set *far* beyond the current situation.

Why then is it not good to set a goal such as "annual income of $80,000" and "TOEIC score of 600" that you seemingly will be able to attain with some added effort? Because as I said before, the brain loves to maintain the status quo. From the perspective of your brain a new goal set just a little higher than the current situation is nothing but a continuation of the status quo.

When the brain judges that we can essentially do as we have been doing in attaining this level of the goal, there is not sufficient energy generated to change the status quo.

Remember "the status quo = the comfort zone." Thus, no activities in the brain will take place to achieve the goal if the goal is not high enough; thus, the goal will not likely be reached.

On the other hand, if the goal is something like "$500,000 annual income" or "TOEIC 950," which seems clearly unattainable at the present time, it would be impossible to achieve this as an extension of the current status quo.

Consequently, the brain starts to think outside of the current situation, and you can expect a big leap in your idea generation capacity. Thus, it is possible to come up with a winning idea on a different plane from your present reality, which can lead to achieving your desired results.

The expression I use above "on a different plane" is like an image that you are going up and through clouds. When you look down to the ground from the clouds, you can get an extensive view of the whole scenery.

Similarly, when you set a high goal, you will notice how narrow your current status is, as well as how little you have been seeing due to your many blind spots. This awareness helps you understand the true nature of things and find a breakthrough—one which no one thought about before.

Such a breakthrough is called innovation. We already mentioned some examples of this when we discussed Steve Jobs. Never before did we have anything like an iPad or an iPhone.

What do I mean by "transcend and break through the status quo?"

It means that you first go above and stand on the ceiling (the clouds), of your current existence, the one in which you are currently living. Secondly, you use the ceiling as a springboard, and you jump higher still.

Whenever you find the phrase, "transcend and break through the status quo," I hope you will imprint in your brain the image of this powerful two-step action—going above the ceiling and jumping still farther up.

Avoid Developing the Burnout Syndrome

Just like you can shoot a rubber band farther by stretching it back more, you can generate more energy toward a goal farther away than a goal close to you. The brain starts functioning for achieving the goal when you set a high, seemingly unattainable one more than when the goal is within your reach.

Moreover, as you get closer to your goal, the energy to get there weakens; thus, it is necessary to renew and reset your goal before achieving the original goal. If not, you may end up getting the so-called "burnout syndrome," as you are unable to generate sufficient energy for achieving the goal. When the goal is as low as your reach, the energy dries up as you get closer to it.

On the other hand, if you constantly set a high goal, the energy generated is ample for moving toward it; thus, you have no time to fall into the "burnout syndrome." As you get closer to the goal, what is important for generating more energy is to find a new high goal, not to stand still.

It is minor detail, but people tend to feel a sense of ease and a sense of being finished, when they have achieved an important goal. We need to be mindful that the feeling of ease inevitably brings with it a sense of maintaining the status quo. This makes it difficult to generate energy to move toward a new goal.

Why an Annual Income of $250,000 Cannot be a Goal?

When you set a goal, I want you to be always aware whether it is truly outside of your current situation. $250,000 might seem high compared to your current income, but it is probably not really widely outside.

If you are working in a company, and if you continue to work there and are promoted steadily, there is a chance that you will one day become the president. If you become president, it is quite achievable to earn this much and more.

I don't mean to imply that it is easy or a simple task to become president, but I do consider getting promoted to be president to be an extension of the current situation, as it is possible to reach this goal by working toward it step by step. It is no exaggeration to say that becoming a president is in the realm of probability.

If your goal is to climb up to be a president, simply because it is a position of high social status, it is not Gold Vision as we are describing it here, because it does not transcend and break through the status quo.

Another all-important question is whether the goal is what you really want to do from the bottom of your heart.

Just chasing after an annual income of $500,000 is meaningless. Let's assume you attain $500,000 through winning a lottery, does it really mean that you have achieved your goal? This applies to the case of "TOEIC 950" in the same way. Even if you get a high score, it will lead to self-complacency, if you don't have a goal for what you want to do with your proficient English.

Now then, what if your goal from the bottom of your heart is "to start a business and earn $500,000 a year—and that is really what you want to do." Or, what if your goal is "to get a job that requires traveling overseas every month, for which you want to achieve the level of TOEIC 950." You will be more motivated to study English compared to the situation where you just want to get the score of 950 as a goal in and of itself. By strongly imagining yourself working overseas, you would generate higher energy for learning English.

In short, you need only two things for enlisting your brain's capacity to work toward materializing your goal.

- Set a good goal that is well outside of the current status quo of your life and that represents something your heart really wants.
- Increase the sense of reality in the desired new "comfort zone" envisioning your goal has been achieved.

When you set a goal far beyond the status quo and you increase the sense of reality in the world of your goal, your priorities will change. Unconsciously, the brain thinks: "There Is no way to achieve the goal in my life as it is now." It starts to generate the necessary energy toward the goal. You will start to see only the important things for materializing the goal through the filtering function of the RAS.

When your sense of reality in the comfort zone is higher in the world of your goal than in the status quo, the brain moves toward the desired goal with its full power.

Make "Subconscious-Me"³ Your Ally

"Subconscious-Me" is the nickname for the subconscious entity that resides inside us.

The important point here is that the brain unconsciously recognizes that there is no way to achieve your new goal as your life and reality are now.

The status quo is what rules in our lives. Thinking unconsciously can be said to be the state naturally brought about, even when we are not thinking consciously. For example,

---

3 "Subconscious-Me" is the English nickname translated for "Muishiki-kun," the Japanese nickname the author gave to the subconscious—another you. While we hope it to be our ally, it often unintentionally behaves like an enemy, especially in achieving our goal.

when we breathe, we are not always conscious of it. The heart is beating unconsciously; it is not something we generally control.

In the same manner, you want to have the brain feel the world of your goal is already real and start moving spontaneously toward it. This unconsciousness is something you might want to call "Subconscious-Me." This is another aspect of yourself, so to speak. In order to achieve the goal, you need to make this "Subconscious-Me" your ally in your Gold Vision process.

It is often the case that the more you want to make money or sell more, you end up in fact not achieving the desired end. It is because your "Subconscious-Me" recognizes your true comfort zone to be "lack of making money" and "lack of selling more." This is your identity, we might say.

Conversely, what you need to do is to make your "Subconscious-Me" believe in "It is natural for me to earn a lot," or "It is natural for me to sell a lot." If the reality is different, then the brain will automatically think that the current situation is unlike what you are. This gap will create strong energy and movement to help you become what you think you are.

In this connection, your "Subconscious-Me" is not convinced when you just say to yourself, "I am determined to make money!" or "I am determined to sell well!" What is important here is to be in the state of mind where "making money" and "selling well" is as natural as your breathing and your heartbeat.

How do we convince our "Subconscious-Me" to support our success in Gold Vision?

Please first begin to become aware of the existence of your "Subconscious-Me."

One of the most effective methods to do so is to engage in regular self-talks. Self-talks are the words that you use to talk to yourself. I will discuss self-talks as well as additional methods to become conscious of "Subconscious-Me" in Chapter 5.

Summary

- To achieve a Gold Vision goal, it is important to set a good goal. We then need to enhance the sense of reality in the comfort zone of the goal world.
- To transcend and break through the status quo, it is important to make "Subconscious-Me" your ally in your Gold Vision process.

CHAPTER 3

Good Goals, Bad Goals

Three Necessary Axes for Setting a Goal—Greatness, Wanting To, and Many

Many of you may be thinking that you must work hard to achieve a particular goal, or it is better to limit the number of goals you set. This is not true. You can achieve a goal without working hard, and you can live a happier life when you have many goals. In this chapter, I will explain the reasons for this.

In Chapter 2, I talked about the importance of setting your goal outside of your current situation. How do we go about doing this?

In fact, it is extremely difficult for us to set a goal outside of our current situation, which is our comfort zone. That's why Disney and Jobs, who did that were indeed geniuses. Some of my clients even say that finding a goal is their goal. It is natural for us to feel uncertain how to set a goal beyond our current situation.

For this reason, Gold Vision recommends thinking in terms of three axes—"greatness," "wanting to," and "many."

Thinking About the Axis of Greatness

"The axis of greatness" means making a goal outside of the current situation. How can we set our goal far away from the status quo? Let's discuss it using some examples.

The simplest method is to increase the number involved. Perhaps you can easily imagine setting a goal far away from your status quo by moving your intended income or assets up by one- or two-digit places from the current level, e.g., increasing 10- or 100-fold. Another example of increasing the number can be seen in getting a greater number of friends.

Some other ways to use the axis of greatness include to extend the length involved, for example, dramatically increasing your life expectancy or active service at work.

A better method for the axis of greatness is to raise "the levels of abstraction" for the goal.

"The levels of abstraction" is an important concept in cognitive science. It refers to the degree of information volume within a subsumptive relation. Simply put, it means how abstract you make things. By raising the levels of abstraction, you will gain a viewpoint higher than before and grasp things more abstractly.

Here are some examples of making the goal in the axis of greatness by raising the levels of abstraction.

Let's suppose your goal is becoming the president of the company you currently work in. It may seem like this goal represents the axis of greatness, but it doesn't.

While it is respectable to aim for higher positions and to do bigger jobs, whether you get promoted to the highest position in the company is to a certain extent a matter of probability.

Theoretically everybody has a chance, however slim it may be. Thus, this goal is sort of an *extension* of the status quo, and it is on "the axis of insignificant greatness," so to speak. Achieving this goal would require of you extra efforts and possibly to go back to school to gain a degree; nevertheless, you already belong to the company, and so you have a chance.

Let's compare "becoming the president" with "working to change the industry." Obviously, the latter is the one that is outside of the status quo, and your goal advances on the axis of greatness.

As the level of abstraction goes up higher, the number of people who will be influenced increases.

For example, a goal of "getting a certificate and enhancing my work performance" could be raised to "mastering the field and creating a certification system myself." In this way, you can expect to influence more people; thus, your goal is getting more aligned with the axis of greatness.

Of course, it is possible for you to make the goal in line with the axis of greatness by simply increasing the number. For example, you can do so by changing your goal from "live well to 70 years of age" to "live well to 100 years of age."

Or your hobby may be music, and you may be wanting to "perform at a live venue." In such a case, your goal climbs up the axis of greatness by changing it to "perform live music every month with top-level musicians at a live location big enough to seat 500 people."

For an exercise, I encourage you to revise your preliminary goals that you have now to ones that move higher on the axis of greatness. You may not be able to get it right away, but you will gradually find what is important to you and start seeing "your Gold Vision distant from the status quo" as if it were a twinkling light between the clouds.

After you tried this exercise many times, you may find a goal that feels good for you. You need to make sure it is indeed in line with the of greatness.

A method to judge whether the goal is really beyond your status quo is to pay attention whether you can see a path forward to materializing it. The concept is very simple. If you readily can identify a way to achieve your goal, it is still within your status quo. If you have absolutely no idea how to achieve it, the goal is more likely outside of the status quo.

Let's assume that you want to go to Tokyo, to Abu Dhabi, or to the South Pole. Even if you have never been there, you can imagine how to get there. Thus, these destinations are considered as part of the status quo. On the other hand, what if you want to go to Mars or Jupiter. Most people don't know how to get there. If so, the goal is outside of the status quo.

Generate Strong Power with "My Things"—"The Axis of Wanting To"

There are techniques to help you set your goal outside the status quo, but it still may be challenging to do it. So, let's make the goal tentative at first, a sort of provisional goal.

Start with what you want to do, "the axis of wanting to." As mentioned in the section discussing particular goals, such as earning an income of $500,000 or a TOEIC of 950, the numbers themselves are meaningless. The important thing is how to achieve the goals. Even if you earned an annual income of $1,000,000, you would not feel happy if it was a result obtained through work you hated to do.

On the other hand, when you are involved in what you really want to do, the brain gets activated and generates energy. If your goal is in line with what you want to do from your heart, you naturally behave accordingly, without any teeth-clenching kind of effort.

When children are absorbed in playing, they are not working hard at all. They literally roll around forgetting everything else.

In the case of an adult, if someone plans to engage in a favorite pastime, e.g., golfing which often requires you to wake up earlier than usual, you naturally wake up without needing an alarm clock. Because you want to play golf as soon as possible, you would not feel that getting up early was a burden.

Let's look at an example in a company. There are cases when the president of a large company made mistakes running the business, neglecting important changes in the surrounding environment despite their knowledge, skills, and talent.

I suspect that in such a case, the mistake is not simply because the size of the company is too big to oversee everything, but rather because the president is not doing what they really want to do. Such presidents who have climbed up the ladder of business success and have been promoted to the president's position are indeed highly capable people.

Nevertheless, they can still overlook crucial issues and details, resulting in various corporate crises. This may be because their goal was to become a president and because running the company was not their most important goal. Since the initial goal of becoming the president was achieved, their brain fell into the status quo mode and stopped generating energy.

When a president operates their business in the "have to" mode rather than the "want to" mode, I believe the RAS does not function properly and develops a scotoma (blind spot), resulting in them overlooking important aspects of their job and thus jeopardizing the company's very existence.

On the other hand, presidents who actually founded companies typically are in the process of achieving the goal they want to achieve, i.e., building a successful company. They are doing what they want to do, and thus regardless of their company's size, most of these presidents do not overlook crucial changes in the environment and instead deal with them properly. Different from some presidents who were promoted through the corporate ladder, the founding presidents are most likely doing what they want to do, not what they have to do.

Whether it is work or study, we experience more energy and attain better results when we engage in the activities that we want to do. Furthermore, when we are doing what we really want to do, our daily life and our goals become more aligned. In this situation, it is more highly probable that our "Subconscious-Me" will pick up on important information that is necessary for our success.

I want to add one more point. If you continue to do what you "don't want to," positive energy is hard to generate, because your state of mind is furthermore negative than that of "have to."

A client of mine who was in his 40s came to see me for coaching. He commented that he was fed up with his colleagues flattering their bosses, hoping to get ahead in the company, or senior members clinging to the company even though they were transferred to a position they did not want.

The reason he wanted coaching was his realization that he did not want to live his life like them, just holding on until retirement age. This client was aware of how badly the influence of continuing to do what he didn't want might affect him in the long-term.

There is an expression, "doing my thing." This refers to something you really want to do from the bottom of your heart. Finding "your thing" makes you powerful more than you can imagine. You don't need to keep living with "have to" and "don't want to" matters and duties. Let's aim instead at the things that you truly want to do.

Is it Really Okay to Do Only What you Want to Do?

Many of you readers might have felt this way as you've read what I've written so far: "I get the point, but I have my real life to live. If I only do what I truly want to do, my family will suffer, because I won't earn enough money to support them."

This is how I myself once thought, so I understand the sentiment. I am not advising you to suddenly drop everything and do only what you really want to. There is more to it than that.

When you make up your mind to live everyday doing what you truly want and set your goal outside of the status quo, you will discover yourself to be quite a different person from yesterday.

What you need is to gradually increase the time you spend doing what you want. Once you set your goal, your life will surely take you closer to it. What you need is to keep on going.

As they refine their goals in line with the axis of wanting to, some of my clients arrive at the intermediate goal of becoming independent and starting a new business. In such a case, I check their self-assurance at the subconsciousness level. When their power of believing in themselves is not sufficient, I recommend that they first cultivate the necessary follow-through power.

You may argue such advice might dampen their motivation upon finding their axis of wanting to after considerable effort. Whether or not you succeed depends on the level of your power to believe in yourself, while you pursue your goal of the axis of wanting to. (Chapter 5 will explain it more in detail.)

Thus, this confirmation cannot be skipped. Even after you set your goal in line with the axis of wanting to, it does not mean all you have to do is rush forward in a straight line.

Let me repeat, it is not necessary to drop everything of your "have tos" all at once. You should keep doing those things necessary for safeguarding your current life.

As you increase the ratio of "want to" to "have to," one day you will arrive at the world where all you do are "want tos." Speaking for myself as an example, all I do now are "want tos." For sure, I was not like this from the beginning.

How to Find Gold Vision—My Sessions With Clients

In this section, I will share some sample sessions with a client for a glimpse into the process of how they came up with their Gold Vision.

Absolutely, securing confidentiality is crucial for coaching. What I want to emphasize here is that the conversations shown below do not belong to a specific individual, rather it is a generalized version of many sessions.

At the First Session:

Client A (**A** hereafter): I have been feeling hazy.

Hisano (**H** hereafter): OK. What do you think is behind that?

A: I have worked in this company for a long time, been promoted, and my income grew to a certain degree, but I cannot see my future.

H: I understand. What do you really want to do?

A: What do I really want to do? (thinking for a while), I have never thought about it.

H: I see. Well, but you are talking to me now. Probably you want to do something about it.

A: Yes, I think so.

H: Let's not rush it. Let's think about it deliberately. I am sure you will find it.

A: Is that how it works?

H: Yes, that's how it works.

A: OK, I won't rush. I'll think it through carefully.

The Second Session, a Month Later:

A: Mr. Hisano, things are getting clearer.

H: Good. How are they now?

A: While I was updating my goals, things got clearer. Please look at this. (He is bringing out a sheet of paper with his goals written.)

H: I see. Your goal before was becoming the first to be promoted to an executive position from among the colleagues who joined the company at the same time[4]. But it is changed now to creating your own business, which you originally wanted to start after retirement. Now, rather than waiting for retirement, you want to start it soon.

A: Yes. While I was thinking of setting a goal that I really wanted from the bottom of my heart, I came to the realization that I am not working for the company but rather I am living my life.

In fact, I was envisioning the business that I was thinking of doing after my retirement, but it was a mere dream for after retirement.

However, when I thought about my goal, I could see what I really wanted to do, and I noticed that they are around this dream of running my own business. Then,

---

4 It is customary in Japan that many large companies hire hundreds of new university graduates right after their graduation at the same school year. Thus, their competition (and camaraderie) exists for 20-30 years.

I realized that there was no reason to wait until my retirement.

H: I see. I understand.

A: Of course, I thought about my option to stay in the company until my retirement age, as I have worked so hard with my job. But I questioned myself about continuing to do what my heart does not desire. As a possibility, I am also looking into other job opportunities. Because I now have a clear goal, I feel everything will align with it.

H: You set a wanting-to goal and you made great strides! That's wonderful!

A: Yes! After I wrote this goal, many ideas came to me. Mr. X is the first person who started this business in Japan. I was thinking about how I could meet him. To my surprise, he was a friend of my client! So, I asked the client to introduce me to him, and he readily agreed to my request. We are now going to meet for dinner next month!

H: Wow, what great progress!

A: Indeed, owing to you, Mr. Hisano! Thank you very much.

H: I am happy for you. All I really did was drink coffee here. (laughter)

A: Not so. You, Mr. Hisano, taught me many things. While I was thinking about updating my goals, I happened to see this goal. The path reveals itself in such a way, doesn't it?

H: That's right. It's simple, isn't it?

A: I don't know if it is simple, but it went so well this time.

H: Indeed. Then, I will help you move ahead.

A: Really? What's that?

H: I want you to meet Mr. X with the intent to be his business partner at the very onset.

A: Really? But he is really far ahead of me.

H: I know, but that is about the past, isn't it? I am talking about the future. Is there any problem if you become a business partner on an equal footing? When you meet someone with such a Gold Vision, your thought will be conveyed at the subconscious level. He will respect you.

A: I see. That's very profound.

H: Yes. You will understand as you get accustomed to it. That's how the things work.

Having pursued the axis of wanting to, this client of mine ended up finding his own goal.

My advice for him to transcend and breakthrough the status quo was to meet with this person who is quite senior to him as if he were a business partner on an equal footing. In this manner, the goal continues to be updated further to a higher level.

In the similar manner, I carry out many conversations with my clients daily. I focus only on the most recent goal of the client; therefore, I don't remember every detail that they said before. Though the pattern of the coaching session may differ, all the session contents are practically the same from the viewpoint of finding goals.

Some clients worry and say, "This is my third session, but I cannot find my goals yet." There is no need to rush. From my experience, I am certain that such people can find "their genuine thing" by the fourth or fifth session. When they leave the session, all of them look so cheerful, feeling delighted in finding their own goal.

There is no "Right Answer" in Gold Vision.

In Gold Vision, there is no such a thing as the "one right answer," which is universally applicable to every person. Somebody's Gold Vision might be to work on something that changes an entire industry. Another person's Gold Vision might be to perform a live session with a top-level musician. What makes a goal that is "beyond the status quo" differs person to person, and only that individual can know it. Thus, other people cannot tell you what kind of Gold Vision is good for you. You must find your own Gold Vision.

You may begin looking into what you really want to pursue by asking questions of yourself. "What is most important to me?" "Will what I thought important in the past be the same for the rest of my life?" "There are things I gave up, thinking there was no chance I could do because of my age (or capability). Will it be possible to make them happen if I figure out a way?"

While you are looking into what you really want to, you will notice your own Gold Vision start to reveal itself. Even if other people think your Gold Vision is trivial or not important, it doesn't matter. Regardless of what they think, the value of your Gold Vision is unshakable to you.

The world in general may value high income and career success, (such a value itself may be a problem, as I will discuss later), but your importance may be making a contribution to society rather than financial success. If so, you would feel great pride and confidence no matter what others say about your Gold Vision.

All my coaching clients say unanimously that they clearly knew "that's it" when they arrived at their own Gold Vision. One of my clients told me he felt, "I'm finally behind the steering wheel of my life. I mean I now feel I can go in any direction I want to."

Does it sound exaggerated? For many people this realization is profound, as they have unconsciously given priority to aligning themselves with the values of their parents and the people around them. They have not been able to live their lives in the way they really wanted to.

Clients commonly tell me: "Since I found my Gold Vision, what I see and what I feel have changed completely. Things started to fall into place and move in the direction that they are supposed to. This is totally different from what I used to feel. I'm no longer in someone else's boat, just dully drifting along. I have found my own direction and I am in charge."

The joy of finding your own Gold Vision can be said to be the happiness you feel from gaining your life's purpose—like the client who says: "I am very happy now and I will always be," I hope that many readers end up feeling this way after following the path laid out in this book.

With the Axis of Many, Make Your Whole Life Happy

"The axis of many" is the third axis and literally means setting many goals.

When I say this many people are surprised. Somehow, they seem to have a preconception of goal = work. Of course, a career goal is important. However, that is not sufficient at all.

To get familiar with this concept of "the axis of many," I recommend my clients to list up at least 100 things that they want to do. In fact, when I was in my mid-20s, I wrote down 300 things. They were something like these:

- Start up and manage a business that I want to do from the bottom of my heart.
- Become a professional in management.

- Manage to have enough free time.
- Live my life without financial worries.
- Become a friend of eminent people.
- Live near a big and beautiful park.
- Have my own website.
- Publish a book.
- Become a person from whom statesmen seek advice.
- Speak fluent English.
- Maintain my physical health and fitness.
- Become the kindest person in the world.

By my mid-40s, the time of this writing, I have materialized 90% of what I wrote down, including the above. The remaining 10% that I was not able to realize were things like these:

- Own a private jet.
- Build a swimming pool at home.
- Hire a private chef.
- Live in a skyscraper.
- Learn tap-dancing.

Later, I found these were not so important to me anymore. Therefore, I can say 100% of what I wanted came true.

Why, then, isn't it good to have only one goal? Of course, I do not deny the idea of dedicating oneself to one thing and mastering the subject. However, life consists of many factors, such as work, family, friends, hobbies, and social contributions. Will you call it a happy life when you achieve one thing, but all the other aspects are not good?

An example may be a gifted professional athlete who achieved an overwhelming success in their sport and took the world by storm. Even a super athlete with exceptional abilities and world records can have difficulty getting out of a slump and being stuck in long-time stagnation. Due to the lack of work/life balance such an athlete may end up destroying his family and being hit by a storm of scandal.

Not only celebrities, like the above example, seem to fall from grace, but also the workaholic employees during the high economic growth period in Japan seemed to have suffered the same fate.

They might have had satisfaction in their jobs. While they were so absorbed in their work, though, they neglected their families. Consequently, there are many who end up losing their goals after retirement and just idle their time away alone without family or friends, and in more extreme cases, they live their lives sad and lonely after their family relationships broke from their neglecting the family for a long time.

The example of workaholic employees is not just somebody else's affair. The companies I coach include some world-famous companies that everyone knows. As a matter of fact, quite a few employees of those client companies have a hard time thinking about goals other than business goals. If you are one of them, I recommend you start coming up with goals outside of work.

Your goals need to cover many aspects of your life, and you need to establish as many goals as possible. To begin with, I recommend listing up at least eight areas that are important to you. If possible, you may want to double the number to 16 and set a goal for each one of them. To better organize your thoughts, you might find it helpful using the balance wheel as shown in Figure 3-1.

Generally, you could easily come up with eight areas such as occupation, family, health, friend, hobby, money, social contribution, and culture.

Some people may include pets, faith, and community. Moreover, it is possible to further breakdown each area. For example, "family" may be broken down to "spouse," "children," and "parents."

By creating a balance wheel, those who initially could only think of goals such as "get promoted in the company and become the president" and "save $1,000,000" expand their goals such as "visit all the world heritage sites (travel)," "make friends outside of the company (friend)," and "begin poetry (hobby)." As their occupational goals grow, the other goals such as hobby and culture also synergistically progress.

One thing I point out is to separate "occupation" and "money." Many people often get lost in confusion in the equation "work = company = money." However, work does not equal money, not to mention, company. Work and occupation mean something similar; I often use "occupation" over "work," as many people tend to strongly associate work with income.

- Each of my children is growing up individualistically, carefree and with peace of mind.
- My spouse is always healthy and happy.
- My parents are enjoying their senior life with peace of mind.
- My family is always filled with smiles.

- I keep developing products and services that the customers really want.
- I am the one and only person in the field, as I have deepened my professional expertise.
- I am happily working, because I found the occupation that I truly want to do.

- Bicycling: I go on a cycling tour twice a year in spring and fall.
- Golfing: I enjoy playing golf twice a month and improving my score steadily.
- Traveling: I visit a few places every year where I want to go on the spur of the moment without time constraints.

- I am contributing $X every month to Organization Y.
- I am participating regularly in social service activities requiring physical labor.

Family   **Occupation**

Hobbies

Social Contributions

Friends

Finances

Health

Culture

- I am earning an annual income of $X through the work I enjoy from the bottom of my heart.
- I am building assets according to my plan to build $Y by a certain point of time in the future.

- I am enjoying the time with my domestic and overseas friends in a wide range of age groups.
- I am expanding the circle of my friends as people come and join the enjoyable events I plan together with my friends.

- I am reading 200 books a year of the fields I am interested in.
- I am going to school to learn about the fields I am interested in.

- I am daily eating the foods that are good for my body.
- I am getting enough sleep everyday to be able to carry out my daily activities with good energy.
- I am setting aside adequate time to relax and pay attention to my own needs.

Occupation is an activity to provide value to the society, and preferably it is in line with what you want to do. Of course, you may be rewarded with money for your activities, but it does not merely mean the money itself. There may be cases in which you receive little or no money.

As for money, it means currency, but it broadly means income, expense, asset, as well as the activities that make the flow of money possible. In this sense, finance may be a better word. For those who feel the term finance unfamiliar, the term money may be used. For example, if you have an activity that is not what you want to do, but you do for your livelihood, it may be better to organize your goal under the category "money" (or finance).

A client of mine works as a clerical worker during the day and trains himself to be a leatherworker for his future independent business during the nights and on weekends. The monetary return that he gets at this stage through leatherwork is minimal, but his activity is undoubtedly creating value for the society. Such an activity may be better organized under the category "occupation."

Of course, the goal for each area should be outside of the current situation. By writing down your goals, you can expect your brain to put up an antenna to start collecting necessary information.

It is recommend that you place these written goals up and see them many times a day. While those goals that you need to see often, so as not to forget, as I will discuss later, may not be the goals that you desire from the bottom of your heart. But it is effective at the beginning to see the goals often to instill them into your subconsciousness.

As each of your goals set from the "axis of many" is materialized, your satisfaction level in life will be enhanced. Don't you feel excited by imaging your life where many of what your heart desires come true?

Does a Currently Happy Person Need a Goal?

Once a person who attended my class said, "I understood well the importance of setting goals beyond the status quo. However, I now feel satisfied and happy with my work, family, and hobby. Do I need to set new goals?"

It is wonderful to feel happy now, however, my answer to this question is "YES." When your goal is achieved, your energy drops down very quickly. Even if you are very happy, your energy goes down rapidly if you are just maintaining the current status quo. If your tomorrow is just like today, it is like subsiding land.

Simply speaking, as you get older, your health is not the same as in your youth and your surroundings also change; thus, maintaining the status quo with doing nothing new is a hard reality. Therefore, it is desirable for even a happy person as well to set goals higher than the status quo.

Of course, if your desire is truly to maintain the status quo, nothing is wrong with that. However, it is questionable that those who feel happiness now just want to maintain the status quo.

If they want to grow further or to enhance themselves,

I hope that they, too, find a goal worthy of betting their lives on.

I heard of data showing a shortened lifespan among those who did not set any goals after their retirement. To live life fully until the very end of life, it is necessary to continuously update your life goals.

Three Powers Needed for Gold Vision

This chapter has a focus on the topic of: "What is a good goal?" Once you set a good goal, what you need to do next is to start moving toward achieving it.

There is one thing I would like you to remember. For many of us our "habitual way of thinking" actually gets in the way of us achieving our goals. In coaching, this is called our "belief system." The habitual thinking often ties us firmly down in our current comfort zone and strongly prevents us from achieving the desired goal.

Our habitual way of thinking is formed in the process of our living. It is fortified especially by three criteria— "money," "time," and "other people." Many people's minds are occupied by their habitual thoughts. This makes it difficult to see even what they really want to do.

Therefore, we need to untangle our habitual thoughts, which is like a ball of tangled yarn, little by little and then we can find our true goals. To reform our standards of "money," "time," and "other people" and make them suitable for achieving our Gold Vision, we need the following three powers.

- The power to see the future.
- The power to believe in yourself.
- The power to involve and move people.

The first item, "the power to see the future" is called imagination. It is the power to set a Gold Vision and feel the sense of reality of being in the world of your Gold Vision.

The second item "the power to believe in yourself" is self-efficacy. It is the power to firmly believe in yourself. It is the conviction: "I can do it."

The third item, "the power to involve and move people" is indispensable for you to take actions toward achieving your goal. More specifically, it is the power to be trusted and supported by others by having them resonate with your Gold Vision.

With these three powers, "the power to see the future," "the power to believe in yourself," and "the power to involve and move people," you can achieve your Gold Vision. In the following chapters, I will introduce how to acquire and utilize these important powers.

Summary

- Bad goals are ones in which you can readily see a path to achieve them.
- Good goals are the ones that you arrive at from the three axes: "the axis of greatness," "the axis of wanting to," and "the axis of many."

CHAPTER 4

"Future Memories" Become Goals

The First Power: The Power to See the Future

See and Feel Your Goal

"The power to see the future," the first power of the three powers[5] to achieve Gold Vision, is to see and feel the goal. What does it actually mean to see and feel your goal?

Let's begin with the word "see." It is essential to set a

---

5 Three powers needed for achieving your Gold Vision are "the power to see the future," "the power to believe in yourself," and "the power to involve and move people."

high goal, as we have already discussed. This is because the higher your goal, the more your world will be widened.

Let's take a simple example. If you compare your view of the world looking down and seeing your feet to that of raising your head and seeing far into the distance, you will notice how radical the difference is. What you see with this shift in perspective is a totally different world. A high goal broadens your view so that you see more.

Recognizing that "your goal = your future," helps you to clearly imagine yourself being in the world of your goal. This is to enhance your sense of reality in the world of the goal, which is deeply related to the aspect of "feel." When you can see your future that way, the brain naturally starts figuring out what must be done to get there.

However, it is not so easy to see the future. When you don't see the future, you tend to easily feel anxious because of uncertainty. Well then, how can we set about seeing the future of our high goal?

To me "the power to see the future" is to create what I call "the memories of the future." If you thought that "memory" means "the past," you are likely subconsciously fixated on the standard view of time as a linear flow from the past to the present and then to the future. This view of time is one of the thinking habits that will get in the way of your Gold Vision. It binds us to the past and distracts us from seeing the future we want to create.

For example, do you normally think this way?

"I studied hard and as a result I passed the test."

Or: "Because I failed that test, I am not living the life I want."

We tend to think like this as a matter of course. I call this "the spell of cause-and-effect relationships."

In fact, you will not necessarily pass the test, even if you study very hard. No matter how hard you studied, if you got sick and had a high fever on the day of the test, you won't be able to show your full capacity. If you are late to get to the test site, because of a public transportation delay caused by a traffic accident, you won't be able to even take the test.

You might have passed your test just because it had questions that you happened to have studied well and got a high score. If the questions covered material that you did not study well, you might not have a favorable result. To pass the test, studying hard is a condition, but it is not the only factor. With other conditions met, it is possible for you to pass the test.

Conversely, failing the test is not the reason why your life is not turning out the way you wished it to be, because there are many other possibilities to live your life other than utilizing and applying the knowledge you gained from your studying hard for the test.

The true reason that your life is not turning out the way you wished for may be because you have not updated your goal, because you have been so obsessed with your original goal and your feelings about the test you failed.

When we buy into reasons, such as "I studied hard, and as a result I passed the test;" and "Because I failed that test,

I am not living the life I want;" the other reasons become blind spots, scotoma. In other words, we create our own story biased on our internal beliefs. Since it is the story that we ourselves created, we tend to be convinced by it without any doubt.

Time Flows From the Future

As you develop skill with the power to see the future, this scale of time starts breaking down. What is important is the future, not the past, because you can influence your future, but you cannot change what already happened. What you have planned for your future happens at the present moment and flows into the past.

Let's think about a simple example. Just imagine that today is Wednesday, and you plan something to do in the coming weekend. (1) This means that you made a decision about your "Future." Then the weekend *comes*, and you enjoy that moment. (2) That is the "Present." When the next Monday *comes* the event has been over. (3) It becomes the Past. As you can see in this context deciding about your Future is the cause of what happens at the Present and moves into the Past.

I understand that many of us have been taught that the future will be created because of our current and/or past efforts. However, when we think about the above example, we may start questioning this kind of standard thinking, and we can see the world from a totally different perspective.

Recently, there are many arguments about time in the

field of scientific research. It is often said that time exists separately from space and there is no flow. We can perceive that time comes from the past or the future. It works in both ways.

If you are caught up with the prevailing understanding of time, you may find it difficult at first to build your power to see the future. What might help you is imagining looking up an escalator moving down, where time is coming toward you from the future. Until you get used to it, it might be helpful to repeatedly create this image in your mind.

Why shouldn't you put importance on the past? As discussed earlier a few times, the brain sees the information deemed important by the RAS and makes the rest scotoma.

Moreover, as you remember things, the brain strengthens these memories and enhances their importance. When you set your goal, self-analysis and counseling will defeat your purpose. In search of "who and what you are," you inevitably explore deep into your past and end up remembering forgotten memories.

Because of the way the brain works, the more the past is strengthened the more the brain starts seeing only the past. Thus, it becomes difficult for the brain to see the future. No matter how well you understand the past, it will not lead you to the future.

What is important is a vision of "yourself in the future," a "future memory" of who you want to be. What you need to repeatedly input into your brain is the desired you in the future.

Let's stop prolonging regrets such as, "If I hadn't done such and such, my life might have been so much better." It is meaningless to hold on to the past in this way saying, "If I had done so and so, I now would be such and such." In the first place, there is no purpose to compare your life now with some other life you might have had.

As you start moving toward "yourself in the future," you will begin to understand that the past was not so important. When your present life is satisfactory, you can see things more positively.

For example, you might say to yourself, "The reason I quit XYZ was because I thought my study would be half-finished. My decision at that time was right. If I still want, I can start doing it now." When I say XYZ, it could be anything you gave up in the past, for example, sports and lessons. If you really want to do it now, what you need is just to do it.

As you start moving toward the radiant "yourself in the future," you will start changing your difficult, hurtful memories to ones that were necessary to support the "yourself in the future."

You might have a bitter memory of getting the cold shoulder from your sweetheart. As you get closer to the version of who you want to be, it will change to, "When I was rejected at that time, I was inspired to become different and work on many things to be here now." Such an update of the past is a function of the brain.

The higher the sense of reality about "yourself in the future," the more the brain starts functioning to adjust your relationship with the past to fit your current situation. It automatically reinterprets and resets the past.

Like an escalator moving down, things that have come down and moved to the past will never come back.

We all have options to choose. You can choose to make decisions based on your future goal, or you can do so based on what happened in the past. If you make decisions based on the future goal, the present will not be the accumulation of the past, because what you do/are doing is channeled through your future goal and is not necessarily related to the past. It may be totally different from what happened in the past. In this case the future will be relatively unpredictable.

If you decide things based on the past events, obviously what happens today and will be happening in the future will be in line with what happened in the past. The future will be more predictable.

It is all about your choice whether to think things from the future or the past. However, my suggestion is to look at the future and put less focus on the past. Usually, this approach will create a better future.

A Goal Must Be Written in the Present Tense

When you write up your goals in "the axis of greatness," "the axis of wanting to," and "the axis of many" (explained in Chapter 3), your "Subconscious-Me" will deeply sense the presence of these goals.

When you do this, the most powerful way is to write your goals in the present tense. In general, the proper way to begin the sentence is with "I." For example, you might say, "I am" or "I am doing" rather than "I want to be."

If you want to be healthy at the age of 100, your goal would be written "I <u>am</u> healthy at the age of 100 years old." If you want to work traveling all over the world, it would be "I <u>am</u> working and traveling all over the world." If you want to have economic stability, enabling your family members the financial support to do whatever they want, it would be written, "I <u>have</u> economic stability that allows my family members to do everything they want." If you want to meet someone wonderful, it would be written, "I <u>have met</u> a wonderful person and <u>feel</u> my happiest ever."

To accelerate the process of achieving the goal, you can use affirmations. This is a term used in coaching. (It is a technique that makes one's subconscious feel one is already achieving the goal by verbalizing the world where your goal is accomplished.)

To enhance the sense of reality when your goal is achieved, it is effective to add emotional expressions such as "delighted," "proud," and "happy" to the sentence you have created, describing the world of the goal in the present tense, as explained previously. For example, the affirmations for the goals mentioned above can be written as follows:

"When I am 100 years old, I am extremely happy, as I am healthy and active."

"I am traveling and working all over the world and greatly contributing to society, and I feel proud doing my important work."

"I have economic stability that allows my family members to do everything they want. Because of it, I am living everyday feeling very satisfied."

"I have met a wonderful person, and I am living everyday extremely happy and excited for my future possibilities."

By writing your affirmations meticulously, you can expect to enhance your sense of reality being in the world of your goal. This practice deeply implants the image of what you want to be into the level of the "Subconscious-Me." When our "Subconscious-Me" recognizes something as important, the brain will start working to support it automatically. If you are good at drawing, you might want to draw a picture of your goal like Walt Disney did for his Disneyland. You will be able to imagine yourself in the future more clearly and concretely.

Power of Reciting the Goal in the Morning

After setting your goal and writing the affirmations, it is effective to make it a habit to recite them every morning while your brain is in the relaxed alfa-wave[6] state.

Rather than reading them silently, it is better to read them aloud and let your ears hear what you are saying, so that you can embed them further into your "Subconscious-Me" with the sense of reality in the world of your goal. At times you might want to include the action of a victory pose that helps you clearly imagine the world of the goal. If it is too much to read all your goals and affirmations, you can pick a few each day and change them regularly.

---

6 an electrical rhythm of the brain with a frequency of approximately 8 to 13 cycles per second that is often associated with a state of wakeful relaxation

As for timing, morning is my recommendation. When the day begins, you read aloud, "At the age of 100 years old, I am healthy," or "I have met a wonderful person, and I am happy." Your brain receives the information and makes you feel positive throughout the day.

As for me, every morning I read aloud my affirmations describing the state where my goals are materialized. For example, some are, "As a top-class coach in the world, I am energetically active and feel fulfilled every day." "I feel proud because top executives in the world come and listen to me at my seminars." It helps me feel energized and happy throughout the day.

During the day, you may encounter incidents which irritate you. Even with such an occasion, it is helpful to recite your goals and affirmations, so that you naturally calm down.

Your Own Perspective is Important

So far, I have often used phrases like, "enhance the reality of the goal," or "enhance the sense of reality in the world of the goal." More precisely speaking, the idea is to increase your own sense of reality of being in the comfort zone[7] of your goal.

Because of the brain's mechanism, it does not simultaneously maintain both comfort zones, the current situation and the world of your goal. The brain is likely to choose the comfort zone with its higher sense of reality.

---

7 A comfort zone is a psychological state in which things feel familiar to a person. A similar term "status quo" represents only now but "comfort zone" can be used to represent the future state as well.

Initially, it might be difficult for you to feel the world of your goal as your true comfort zone, especially when you set a high goal. Therefore, the key is to increase the sense of reality in the world of the goal. The point is to imagine the world of the goal from your own perspective.

Let's suppose you are a soccer player, and your goal is to win the World Cup. What kind of images would you see?

One image might be of you bursting into joy with your teammates at the moment of victory. You are smiling and holding the trophy up high. You may see yourself in a championship TV interview. However, all these examples are images viewing yourself from outside. Images like this of TV cameras capturing the soccer win are generally not enough to sufficiently enhance the sense of reality for your new goal.

To raise the sense of reality in yourself being in the world of the goal, it is necessary to imagine the world of the goal seen from inside out. More specifically, it is not the image of you holding up the trophy, but the image you are seeing and the feeling that goes with it while you are holding it. In the case of the interview, you want to imagine the scenery you would be seeing when you are receiving the interview. The more realistically you can imagine, the closer your goal gets to being actualized.

Fully Activate Your Five Senses

When you see the world of the goal subjectively to enhance the sense of reality, it is effective to fully activate your five senses to imagine it, rather than just your visual sense.

Let's take the example of winning the World Cup. Your ears, while you are holding the trophy up, are hearing the spectators in the sold-out stadium shouting for joy. If it is nighttime, your sweaty cheeks might be feeling a pleasant, cool breeze. You might smell the sweat of your teammates after the battle, the smell of green grass in the pitch; you might see the shining lights, the blinding photoflashes; you might feel the hugs of your teammates; you might even taste the saltiness of their tears rolling down their faces. As you imagine more and more precisely, you will feel many more things.

Just like this above example of winning the World Cup, all five senses should be employed fully in your goal process. Please try doing this with your own personal goal and compare how strongly you feel the world of the goal with only visual image vs when you fully activate all five senses.

Extract the Feelings of Success

After you imagined the world of the goal using all five senses fully, next you then add your feelings to it. Because you have not yet arrived at the world of the goal, however, you don't really know how you would feel.

So, what you can do is to remember your past experiences of successes, bring out your emotions and apply them to the world of your goal.

For example, imagine your goal is to succeed with a big project at work. When you try to imagine your feelings of arriving at the world of the goal, recall your earlier experiences of achieving something with colleagues or teammates and of working together. These could be winning the first place in a relay at a track meet or of making an event successful at a cultural festival during your student days. Depending on your past experiences, many successful ones could be listed.

What is important is not the experiences themselves but your own feelings at the moment. In this process, the power to see the future, not the past, is enhanced. In this process we seek to extract only the feelings out of the successful experiences in the past.

When you are seeing things from your own perspective, enhancing your image of the world of your goal with your five senses, and adding your emotions to it, the world goes through a dramatic transformation, as if changing from monochrome to color.

You may call this influence "the power of emotions." Our emotions indeed have a powerful impact on our comfort zone.

Try to Unsettle Your Current Comfort Zone

While we are behaving ordinarily, the brain's tendency is to stay in the status quo. Thus, when we try to change, the power pulling back to the status quo is great. It is like trying to escape the gravitational pull of the earth. To oppose this force, one of the most effective methods is to unsettle the current comfort zone by intentionally experiencing the world of the goal.

If possible, I recommend you to actually visit the world of the goal that you desire and to experience it.

If you are preparing for an entrance examination, you might visit the school you want to attend. By doing so, you will get a clear image of how you are going to live your campus life after entering the school.

If you are an employee and thinking about starting your own business, I encourage you to go a place where entrepreneurs gather and talk to them, rather than just thinking about many things in your mind. Being in the actual physical location increases how real your new goal feels.

If you want to start your own business but you still are one of those 9-to-5 salaried employees, who are surrounded by colleagues reluctantly working, simply because it's their job, you might experience it as a sort of culture shock to meet with people who are enthusiastically talking about their business goals with a gleam in their eyes.

When you get together with these entrepreneurs, you will likely feel that the place you want to be is not in a company where many employees are low spirited. Instead, you desire to be in a place where you can share your own business goals passionately. When you envision your future as an entrepreneur, experiences like this will give you a positive boost.

In this way, when you get a taste of the world of your goal, your current comfort zone is unsettled by recognizing "things are not good as it now is." Moreover, that recognition arises from the subconscious realms; therefore, it will provide you with great propelling power for you to move forward. Experiencing the world of the goal is something that many people recognize is desirable to do, but they somehow don't actually follow through.

However, as discussed earlier in the context of "fully activate your five senses," whether you are there or not makes a big difference. The greater your sense of reality in the world of the goal, the closer you get to achieving the goal. It means we have no other choice but to do it. Without trying, nothing happens.

After you take your action to be there in the physical location of your goal, you might realize, "It wasn't what I thought it to be." Then, what you need is to look for other ways. If you feel, "It is good," you want to continue and to increase the number of such actions.

"Looking at your Goals" as if Brushing Your Teeth

At times people ask me, "Is it better to post my goals where they stand out?" Honestly, if you forget them so easily, probably they are not such important goals for you. The truly valuable goals are what are the ones always in your mind, thus, there is no need to remind yourselves of them with post-it notes on the mirror and such tricks.

The future is not something that you *have to* see in the sense of forcing yourself. It feels more like your "Subconscious-Me" naturally looking at yourself in the future. When your future is visible, you have no other choice but thinking about your goals while waking or sleeping.

For an athlete whose goal is getting a gold medal in the Olympics, it is always in their mind. A doctor whose desire is to help their patients recover their health—they are always thinking about helping their patients. A good teacher is always mindful of, "Are my students growing?" and "What can I do to help them?" A writer is conscious about creating a good piece of work, day-in, day-out. A politician who has their country at heart would be naturally, without being told by anybody, thinking about how to meet the people's needs.

When you start thinking about your goals at the subconscious level, you have really gotten the point. When you look at your goals as naturally as you brush your teeth, you have acquired the power to see the future.

Summary

- "The power to see the future" is the power to have your Gold Vision and to feel the sense of reality in the world of that vision.
- In other words, it is the power to create your "memories of the future."

CHAPTER 5

Create New Circuits in the Brain

The Second Power: The Power to Believe in Yourself

The Reason Why You Cannot Achieve the Goals You Set

As has been repeatedly discussed, setting a high goal is indispensable for achieving your Gold Vision. However, even if you set an appropriate goal in this way, it alone will not be enough to attain it.

Have you ever experienced something like this? You say to yourself, "I can't go on this way anymore; I really want to change." You then try to do one thing after another, but soon you find yourself pulled back to your original status quo. When this pattern occurs, we typically find it depressing, and we say things in our self-talk such as "I'm no good," or "I'm just not the type of person who can change." For sure, if you have an experience like this, it is not because you are no good.

Why did things go wrong then? It is not rare, in fact, that people end up staying locked in the status quo despite setting a high goal.

Let's look at an example of a person who worries, "I won't be able to grow anymore in the company where I work." In this circumstance, let's consider two possible goals we could think of for an employee like this.

- Seek another job with a different company where moving up the ladder of success is possible.
- Leave the company and start a new business of your own.

However, people in this sort of dilemma often start wondering if they should really give up their current job and social status; they start to worry about the future if they jump ship and go to a new employer. Maybe things there will be worse in some ways. In fact, there are many people who are dissatisfied in this way who cannot make up their mind and they end up staying at the current company too scared to make a move.

Another example might be aiming to become fluent in a foreign language. Whether acquiring high language skills is a big goal or not depends on where you start from. In fact, quite a few people want to achieve this, and it is a meaningful target for them to go after. Yet, unfortunately, the reality is that not many of them gain the high proficiency that they envisioned. Of course, we can think of many other examples.

The major reason for being unable to achieve the goal is the existence of what we might call "dream killers." Dream-killers say negative messages to our "Subconscious-Me" such as "No way you can do it."

As the name suggests, dream-killers are those thought patterns that literally kill your dreams. These kinds of dream-killing messages can come from our own self-talk but can also come from your parents, siblings, spouse, other family members, friends, teachers, bosses, and colleagues at work. Anyone can be a dream-killer if they are strongly invested in maintaining the status quo. The higher your goal is, the more the people around you tend to become dream-killers.

As has been explained, we all maintain our comfort zone. Our comfort zone is maintained individually as well as by a group. Setting a high goal and trying to change the status quo means that we are, in effect, confronting the group-maintained status quo. Therefore, when you set a high goal, the "Subconscious-Me" of the people around you will try to maintain the current comfort zone that they have established together with you. Consequently, they end up behaving like dream-killers against you.

The dream-killer phenomenon is an inevitable outgrowth of the forces trying to maintain the comfort zone. Everyone holds within themselves the possibility of becoming a dream killer. To achieve our Gold Vision goal, it is necessary to watch out and beware of the dream-killers around you. On the other hand, we can ourselves be our own greatest dream-killer.

The force of maintaining the comfort zone you have created and maintained over time is more powerful than you can imagine. To achieve your goal, despite this force, it is essential for your "Subconscious-Me" to strongly believe in its materialization in the world of your goal. This is the second power necessary to achieve Gold Vision—"the power to believe in yourself."

From my experiences coaching many people, where the maximum power to believe in oneself is 100%, I feel the minimum requirement is 95% for achieving a goal. With less than 95% power, it is difficult to reach our goals.

Let's assume a client whose level of the power to believe in oneself is 80%. In my assessment, when such a client says, "I want to quit my job and start my own business," I usually advise them to wait a bit and to focus first instead on enhancing their power to believe in themself.

With only 80% confidence, I consider that a client like this is not ready yet for a quantum leap. Just as two wheels of a cart need to work in harmony, both "setting a high goal" and "the power to believe in yourself" are indispensable for materializing your Gold Vision.

At the same time, the relationship between these two aspects is like the proverbial riddle of the "chicken and egg." It is hard to tell which comes first. When a person can set an extremely high goal, they will feel to themselves, "How amazing I am to be able to set such a high goal!" The same person will likely have a high level of "the power to believe in yourself," and will also feel, "Because I have such a great ability, it is natural for me to be able to set a tremendous goal."

What is "The Power to Believe in Yourself"?

"The power to believe in yourself" is equivalent to the term "efficacy" used in coaching. Efficacy is a well-known term used in psychology. It is defined as the self-evaluation of one's abilities to produce desired results. It is often expressed as "self-efficacy."

To put it simply, it is the power to believe confidently and wholeheartedly, "I can do it." The point is to "believe confidently and wholeheartily." Believing confidently and wholeheartily is the state where one is totally believing in oneself in having the abilities to achieve a high goal without even 1% doubt—in other words, believing it at the subconscious level. In the same way that we do not worry about whether the sun will rise tomorrow, it is the state where we take achieving our goals for granted.

After all, you are setting a high goal that you have never

before seen. Therefore, it is contradictory to be able to say with absolute confidence, "I can do it." Nevertheless, it is important to move toward this state of mind. Only then can you expect breakthroughs. There are those who can greatly help you become more self-confident and guide you toward your goal.

For example, a coach might say to you, "If you are going to challenge yourself, why not go all the way to the national championships." Maybe when your coach says this, a fleeting image of yourself being at the championships pops up. In this manner, you are grasping this rapid image which is actually the image of your goal being fulfilled. This is the image of the future version of yourself that you desire to become.

There aren't that many people who can believe in themselves to this extent, i.e., a true 100%. Maybe you have someone in your life who believes in you to this degree; when you encounter someone like this who really believes in you even more than you believe in yourself, then the power to believe in yourself gets a strong boost.

Differences From Those Who Have High Self-Evaluation Only

"The power to believe in yourself" has two conditions. One is a premise of having a goal. The power to believe in yourself is in the context of achieving the goal. It may sound too obvious, but this is an important point.

Having read "believing in yourself" and "high self-evaluation," some readers may be wondering what about those troublesome people who have very high self-evaluation but a low performance. What is the difference between them and those who believe in themselves and actually achieve their goals? The difference lies in whether one has a goal or not.

Having high self-evaluation itself is good of course. However, when it is not supported by actual skills, the balance is off and becomes a problem. Let's assume there is Mr. A, a young employee, who has insufficient capabilities but high self-evaluation. Whether he has a firm goal or not would take him to two distinctly different paths. On one path he would be just a troublesome employee with high self-evaluation and no follow through. On the other path he would actually materialize his goal due to his power to believe in himself.

Generally, those who become troublesome individuals with only high self-evaluation and lacking skills tend to lack clear goals. They are often attracted by a socially acceptable job image, one that is seen as cool and admirable. However, as they are not actually pursuing their goals, they do not know specifically where they need to put their best efforts forward. In this way they stay a high self-evaluation, poor performance person.

On the other hand, when Mr. A has a firm goal, he becomes aware of where he has a deficit in his abilities. Thus, he would put forth the necessary efforts to fill the gap. In this way he ends up becoming a person who can achieve his Gold Vision goal, due to his power to believe in himself.

Setting a goal is required for generating true "power to believe in yourself."

Remove the Standards of Others

The second condition for the power to believe in yourself is the irrelevance of the judgments and standards of others. Here, too, we are presuming the existence of a goal. Goals are different for different people. Everyone has different priorities and values in life and our goals will change depending on these differences. Thus, no two people are exactly the same.

As everyone sets their own goals, it is meaningless to compare and compete with the goals of others. Moreover, what you want in your life is the true basis for setting your goals. Because of this there is no need for others to offer a critique of your goal.

Those who are considered the serious, honor student type of person have a strong tendency to think, "It must be this way or that way," according to the standards set by society. In many cases, they believe their value is determined by the evaluation of the people around them. This type of individual also tends to feel depressed when they feel inferior to others due to comparing themselves with others.

Let's recall the definition of "the power to believe in yourself" is "the self-evaluation of one's own capabilities." The standards are to be set by you and nobody else. Your value is determined by you, not the supervisor, not the president, not your co-workers—just by you. Removing the other people's standards is an important step to generating a strong power to believe in yourself and to think on your own.

You might be able to find around you those who always tend to compare themselves with other people, no matter what the topic is. In fact, whenever you compare yourself with others, you end up hurting yourself. When you evaluate yourself by the standards set by others, you are intrinsically giving up your own steering wheel for your life.

For example, there are some of my clients, who have decided to receive my coaching and then start to question whether they are worthy of such a high-level coaching that Olympic gold medalists receive. There is, of course, no need at all to compare themselves with Olympic gold medalists.

This self-sabotaging thought pattern occurs because their "Subconscious-Me" is trying desperately to maintain the status quo. It typically senses coaching as troublesome because it can dramatically change the status quo. It tries to convince them not to do it.

I often talk to such clients and say the following, "You decided to receive coaching, because you thought you needed it. Although you feel uneasy about it, you came to have a session with me. That itself is evidence you have overcome the status quo to a certain degree."

When I say this, they show a relieved look. This realization eventually leads them to "the power to believe in themselves." They eventually come to the realization, "I am the only one, not anybody else, who can recognize my abilities; only I can take off the limits I placed on myself previously."

Your life is yours. Stop evaluating yourself by the standards set by others and live your life according to your own standards. This is the absolute condition for enhancing "the power to believe in yourself."

Break Your Thought Habits

Previously, I talked about our thought habits that we tend to think, based on three standards, which are just social preconceptions. Here I want to introduce some examples when people are unable to exert "the power to believe in yourself" 100% due to being bound by these three standards:

- Those who earn more money are greater, have more prestige, (money standard).
- I failed before so no way will I succeed this time, (time standard, bound by the past).
- When I was growing up, I was not taken seriously by my parents, so I tend to view myself negatively, (time standard bound by the past and others' standards).
- I cannot think of any other profession for me, except medical doctor, (others' standard, "the best is to become a medical doctor").
- I am no good because I don't have a good academic background, (others' standards, "your value is determined by the school you graduated from" and your time standard clinging to the past).

- I am inferior because I work in a small company, (others' standard, a set hierarchy of companies).
- I cannot go to a good school with such a poor standardized test score, (others' academic standards, and time standard—which is based on the past performance).
- I am afraid of speaking up about what I really think, (others' standards).
- Feeling miserable or superior by comparing yourself to others who came to a class reunion, (mixture of money, time, and others' standards).
- I have to wear fashionable clothes, (others' standards of "comparing yourself with others").
- We must buy a new car or a TV, because the next-door neighbor did, (mixture of others' and money standards).
- People from good family lineages are deemed as praiseworthy, (time standard).

The degree varies, but most of us are bound by these three standards. The kinds of thought habits we might have depend on each individual person, but what is common is that these standards form a scotoma for us and narrow our views. Let's remove the standards from the above examples and see what kind of higher view we can get:

- To live life fully, high goals are more important than high income.

- I will do better this time.
- My parents were not so affirmative of me, but that is irrelevant to my goals.
- Beside becoming a medical doctor, there are many professions that I can pursue and contribute to society.
- Many leaders of the world's businesses do not necessarily have a high academic background. It's irrelevant to what I will accomplish.
- The size of a company is not important. What is important is if I and the company have high goals that enrich our lives and those of others.
- Academic performance can be improved. All I need to do is to put forth my best efforts for my goal.
- It is less stressful to live my life expressing what I genuinely think rather than suppressing it.
- Since our graduation, all of us have lived our lives the best way we could. Let's celebrate together.
- I'll wear whatever clothes I want.
- The neighbor's car (or TV) is wonderful, but do we really need one for our house?
- What kind of family I grew up belongs to the past. How I should live from now on is the important point.

As we take off the standards set by others, we get rid of thinking how we may be viewed socially, and we gain the viewpoint for moving toward what we really think is important and what we really want to do.

These standards are the accumulation of each person's whole life history. Therefore, it is inevitable we will need some time for our "Subconscious-Me" to be free of thought habits.

Even so, when we acquire the knack for getting rid of these standards that come from others, it becomes surprisingly easy to do so.

Among the three standards of "time," "money," and "others," the money standard is relatively easy to remove. If you feel you are strongly possessed by the money standard, you might gather up your courage and tear a 100-dollar bill in half. This act will convince you the money that you were obsessed about was no more than just a piece of paper. In fact, many, including my clients, were successfully able to get rid of the money standard with this method. The effect is proven.

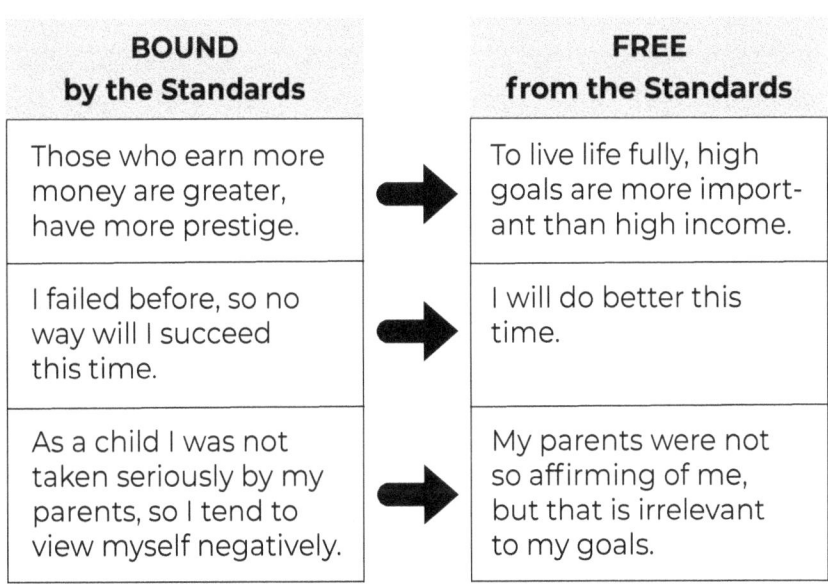

BOUND by the Standards		FREE from the Standards
Those who earn more money are greater, have more prestige.	→	To live life fully, high goals are more important than high income.
I failed before, so no way will I succeed this time.	→	I will do better this time.
As a child I was not taken seriously by my parents, so I tend to view myself negatively.	→	My parents were not so affirming of me, but that is irrelevant to my goals.

Figure 5-1: Remove the standards

Create New Circuits in the Brain With Positive Self-Talk

Self-talk messages are important for taking care of our thought habits. They are the words that you say to yourself both consciously and subconsciously. They include associated thoughts, images, and emotions.

A client of mine told me, "When my self-talk gets better, my confidence is naturally enhanced, and I feel my goal is already more than halfway achieved." I totally agree.

After listening to this comment, I came up with a phrase, "Those who control their self-talk control their lives." It may sound too self-praising, but I believe this phrase is quite good at getting at the heart of the matter. There are two kinds of self-talk, and it is important to understand the characteristics of each kind and become good at dealing with them.

I call these two self-talks "the bubble-up type" and "the imprint type." The term "self-talk" has gained popularity in recent years. However, there seems to be different interpretations and some confusion. However, the categorization into these two types can help organize our understanding of the characteristics of these types of self-talk.

Let's start with "the bubble-up type of self-talk." They are the type of self-talk that pops up in our heads like air-bubbles popping up while water is boiling. From the time that we get up until we go to bed, it is said that we humans have 50,000 self-talk messages a day, including the subconscious ones. Generally, our "Subconscious-Me" is filled with these bubble-up type of self-talk. These bubble-up self-talk messages arise from your "Subconscious-Me," a part of yourself that you cannot control, and they are delivered to your "Conscious-Me," that part of yourself that you can control.

On the other hand, "the imprint type of self-talk" refers to the ones that are consciously created. These are the self-talk messages that you intentionally create to improve the quality of naturally bubbling-up self-talk. Therefore, contrary to the bubble-up type self-talks, the imprint type self-talks are delivered from your "Conscious-Me" to your "Subconscious-Me," so to speak.

As they are consciously created, imprint type self-talk messages are like affirmations, which were introduced in Chapter 4. While affirmations are mainly intended to express the comfort zone of the goal world, imprint type self-talks are the expressions of what you want to be in more common day-to-day situations, although they can include the goal world. These self-talk messages can be considered as lighter than affirmations and for more everyday use.

The imprint type self-talks can be further divided into two subtypes. The first subtype is that you intentionally reverse undesirable bubble-up type self-talks as you recognize them.

Examples:
**Undesirable "bubble-up type" self-talks
to "imprint type" self-talks.**

"Aah! It's no good after all." ➡ "It's not so bad, I can still do it."

"Oh no, I'll be late." ➡ "What can I do now?"

"I am anxious." ➡ "It's natural, as I'm trying it for the first time. I will do my best. It will work out."

The second subtype of "imprint type" self-talk is when you intentionally create favorable self-talks and communicate them to yourself, even though you don't necessarily notice unfavorable "bubble-up type" self-talk messages.

You saturate these self-talks into your "Subconscious-Me," in the hopes that it will become full of positive bubble-up type self-talk. Many athletes often use this imprint type of self-talk during the game. A typical example would be: "Yes, I'm good," as introduced in a Lou Tice's book.

Examples:

"Yes, I can. Yes, I can."

"I am good!"

"Calm down, calm down."

"Believe in me, believe in everyone."

Instill High Quality Self-Talk Into Your "Subconscious-Me"
How then should we deal with each type of self-talk? What we need to understand first is that many negative bubbling-up

self-talk messages reflect a "Subconscious-Me" that is filled with negative thoughts. On the contrary, many positive bubbling-up self-talks reflect a "Subconscious-Me" that is filled with positive thoughts.

Obviously, we want to fill up our "Subconscious-Me" with positive self-talk for achieving our goals. Our "Subconscious-Me" is made up of our past experiences and thought habits, including the bias from the three typical standards.

How can we transform our "Subconscious-Me" into a more desirable one? Specifically, how can we instill high quality "imprint type" self-talk messages into our "Subconscious-Me," so that it can improve the quality of our "bubble-up type" self-talk and naturally move us forward toward the goal?

Every time we experience something, the brain stores it in the neural network. So, enhancing the quality of our self-talk can be imaged as if you are creating a new circuit.

By consciously creating good self-talks, (imprint type self-talk), you are updating your "Subconscious-Me" to make better bubbling-up self-talk messages.

How can we improve the quality of bubbling-up self-talk? The "Subconscious-Me" of those who have not fully developed "the power to believe in yourself" is like a glass of dirty water (filled with bad bubble-up type self-talk messages).

Imagine you put the glass under a water tap in the sink where clear water is dripping. (Here the clear water represents good self-talk messages = imprint-type self-talk.)

As time passes, the dirty water, (bad self-talks = bubble-up-type self-talk), will be replaced by new clean water, (good self-talk = imprint-type self-talk). Thus, the water in the glass ("Subconscious-Me") becomes clean.

When the water in the glass is completely clean, the "Subconscious-Me" is filled with good self-talk for achieving your goal, (bubble-up-type self-talk). Once you reach this level, you can expect to bring the water ("Subconscious-Me") back to the clean state, even if some dirty water comes in from the outside environment.

In the previous section, I talked about two subcategories of imprint-type self-talks. Both are very effective for changing your "Subconscious-Me."

Self-talk Messages Change Lives

One of my clients grew up as a child continuously given negative remarks by his parents. Consequently, he was in severe self-denial thinking: "I should never have been born." "If I didn't exist, it would be better for everyone else." "I am not worthy at all." It must be so hard and difficult to live life with such thoughts. He told me that he often thought, "I hope my life will end soon."

One day he came to see me, wishing to change himself. In the beginning, it was difficult for him to generate positive self-talk messages.

For example, he would attempt to create imprint-type self-talks such as "I am a worthy person," or "I can fulfill what I want." Then, he would immediately have bad self-talks quickly bubbling up saying, "I cannot be worthy," or "No way, no way. It's a waste to try anything."

I told him, "Let's be patient and go slowly. Since you lived your life for decades with such subconsciousness, the change won't be so quick and easy.

However, you can convey positive 'imprint type' self-talks to yourself, and your 'Subconscious-Me' will surely respond. It may feel a long process to you, but if you continue it for two to three months, things will change."

I continued, "Putting positive self-talk messages into your subconsciousness will draw out the exact opposite negative self-talks from the subconsciousness. To maintain the status quo, your subconsciousness brings out the negative self-talk messages to crush your positive thoughts.

Therefore, the more you try your positive self-talks, the more you will feel saddened. However, you must dare to create some confusion like this to clean up your subconsciousness. Otherwise, this negative self-talk is active behind the scenes of your awareness deep inside the subconsciousness and can bring your life downward without you knowing it. Sadly, this has been your life so far."

Listening to these comments from me, he looked greatly shocked. Literally, he was out of breath and speechless.

Even so, I continued further, "However, the past is irrelevant. It's all history. What I am encouraging you to do now is a tried and true and safe method." I told him, "If you continue this process for two to three months, things will get better. So, let's continue. When you get anxious along the way, please contact me at any time."

Through coaching, he replaced negative self-talk habits

with supportive ones, and his "Subconscious-Me" became filled with positive self-talk. About six months after starting coaching, the client would instill imprint-type self-talk messages, such as: "I am a worthy person," and "I can get everything I want." The bubble-up self-talk messages naturally became positive, responding: "Oh, yes. That's right," and "Definitely, I can make it. There is nothing I can't do."

Like this example, when your "Subconscious-Me" affirms you 100% and supports you, the water in the glass, (your subconsciousness), will be completely clean. Now this client says, "Living is not suffering for me anymore." Furthermore, he says, "I feel that living is really fun."

Raise the Purity of Your "Subconscious-Me"

In this connection, those who are considered top coaches all have high purity of their "Subconscious-Me." They recognize their clients' goal achievements as natural without any doubt.

Those clients who move forward with such coaches subconsciously are influenced by the coaches' high purity, and the clients' own "Subconscious-Me" gets cleaner.

The absolute requirement for coaches is that they unconditionally must not become their clients' dream killers. If those coaches whom their clients trust end up pulling them down, it is as if they were getting their priorities backwards.

However, it is easier said than done. The job of a coach is to work for their client's success. Naturally, a comfort zone is formed between the coach and the client. When the client alone becomes successful and progresses ahead, maintaining the comfort zone can become difficult.

Therefore, the coach's subconsciousness tries to stand in the client's way.

This is a physiological phenomenon caused by the brain; it is as natural as sweating when you feel hot. Therefore, it is not something that ordinary people can stop consciously.

Since the comfort zone has this capability, those who want to become coaches need special training for dealing with their subconscious. Only after receiving such training and committing themselves to discipline to never become the client's dream killer, can they become successful coaches who the client feels safe with and to whom they will entrust their future.

Let me summarize: Filling our "Subconscious-Me" with positive self-talk to raise its purity is something similar to a complete game-changer. Once you have it, you become invincible. You fear nothing, even anticipated obstacles for achieving your goal. It is as if you are gaining wings to fly and are able to materialize anything.

Let's Write Down Your Own "Bubble-Up" Type of Self-Talk

I usually give my clients a homework assignment to write down their self-talk messages. Or I sometimes ask the person to write them down during an hour-long session.

The first step is to become aware of your own self-talk. I call this exercise a "self-talk pick-up." Through this simple exercise, you will experience just how many words you generate in your self-talk. You will become more strongly aware of the existence of your "Subconscious-Me."

By all means, I encourage the readers of this book to do the same homework. What kind of self-talk messages are on your list? Here I would like to define more clearly the difference between good (positive) and bad (negative) self-talk.

- Good (positive) self-talk: The ones that lead you toward your goal.

- Bad (negative) self-talk: The ones that lead you away from your goal.

Moreover, please recall, that the goal is something you want to reach or achieve. Therefore, the positive self-talk messages are typically stated, "I want to..." On the other hand, the negative ones are often phrased, "I have to..."

Especially, those who have a lot of self-talk in the form of "I hate to..." must be mindful, because hate-to messages are actually worse than the "have to" type.

By repeatedly instilling this hate message into your "Subconscious-Me," you will end up creating circuits that reinforce your "hate to." The more you repeat self-talk like this, the more you move toward hurting yourself. In the worst-case scenario, no matter what happens, you will become trapped in hostility.

You might notice your self-talk is like: "Every day, I seem to only have difficult things to do," and "My boss will find fault with me again today. I hate it."

If you notice such self-talk going around and around in your head, let's stop this vicious circle. With this viewpoint in mind, I want you to review your self-talks. If you find your self-talks are not so favorable, you can change them with favorable "imprinting type" self-talks. More specifically, in this process you create your self-talks imagining what you would be saying in the world of the goal. Here are some examples:

Example 1:

What happened: Failure.

Bad self-talk: "Oh no! I failed again."

Good self-talk: "Well, what shall I do?"
(Look to the future.)

Example 2:

What happened: Confronted with a challenge.

Bad self-talk: "No way that I can do it."

Good self-talk: "It's alright, I can do it! How should I approach it?" (Look to the future.)

Example 3:

What happened: A colleague joining the same year you did achieved the top sales performance in the company.

Bad self-talk: "He is great, but why I am not good enough?"

Good self-talk: "He is great. I am happy for him. I want to do my best." (Look to the future.)

Example 4:

What happened: You want it, but it's too expensive.

Bad self-talk: "Too expensive! I can never afford the things I really want."

Good self-talk: "It's quite expensive! Do I really need it? If I need it, how can I get it?" (Accept the current situation and look to the future.)

Example 5:

What happened: It's raining.

Bad self-talk: "Damn, it's raining! I hate the rain. It's so cold and damp!"

Good self-talk: "Wow, it's raining. We need the rain so badly. I'll just take my umbrella with me." (Don't mind what you can't do anything about.)

Example 6:

What happened: Strenuous work tired you out.

Bad self-talk: "This darn job is so hard!"

Good self-talk: "I am tired, but it's a good kind of tired." Just say what you feel. (Negative self-talk is a signal from the brain, so, clarify what it is. As a result, you can think of a countermeasure, such as a needed rest because you are tired.)

Next, we will look at some examples for changing the "bubble-up type" self-talk that are framed as "have to" into "want to." In parentheses, the resulting happenings derived from the "want to" self-talks are shown.

"I have to go to work" ➡ "I want to go to work to do what I like." (Remember when you joined

the company because it was the work
you wanted to do.)

"I have to get up." ➡ "I want to get up for myself."
(Reduce staying up late meaninglessly
and go to bed earlier.)

"I have to bring my child up well." ➡ "I want to
do my best for my precious child." (Balance the time
for childcare with securing time for yourself.)

"I have to be friendly with everyone." ➡ "I want to
be close to those with whom I get along well."
(Being sociable becomes fun.)

"I have to sell the way I was trained to do." ➡ "I
want to know about the products and do a good
job conveying their merits to my accounts."
(Sales activities become enjoyable.)

Gain Persevering Power With Self-Talk

Self-talk plays another important role. It can give us the
power to persevere by maintaining the sense of reality in
the comfort zone in the world of the goal. As discussed
earlier, as an animal instinct, the brain strongly seeks to
maintain the status quo. For that purpose, our "Subconscious-Me" attempts to maintain the status quo and disturb
any attempt to break through it toward the goal.

- Your dieting went well, but suddenly a rebound from weight-loss starts happening.
- Although you quit drinking, one day you end up drinking all night long.
- You are prescribed one more treatment for curing your disease, but you don't follow through.
- Everything went well, but somehow you end up contacting someone, who you shouldn't have.
- You are about to go to an event, which is expected to bring you a great success, but you cannot find your wallet.
- Recently, good things happened one after another, but you suddenly get sick.

Besides these examples, you might run into such situations like, "abruptly, you lose motivation," "you become intensely anxious," and "you suddenly get irritated." These phenomena are all the act of your "Subconscious-Me" trying to halt your forward movement toward the goal and bring you back to the status quo.

You might wonder if it really works this way. In fact, the brain is highly creative in using all kinds of means for maintaining the status quo and preventing us from moving forward. The brain's power to maintain the status quo is that strong.

Of course, things are not all bad. When we stumble on something and struggle to get up again, the same power to maintain the status quo works strongly for us. Due to that function, we are protected from big falls.

Even though the brain's power to maintain the status quo has good aspects, the force to repeatedly shake up our smooth progress towards our goal tends to make us feel, "That's right, I knew I couldn't do it." If you take in that kind of self-talk, you are creating a circuit in the brain with the story of the goal you are unable to achieve. The goal you set may be unshakable, but your "power to believe in yourself" may not be.

Here, too, we can use "imprint type" self-talk. When you are in the middle of that turmoil, you feel as if it lasts forever, and you will not be able to move ahead. In such a situation, it is important to not let your negative self-talk control you. What is essential is to aggressively instill "imprint type" self-talk messages, so that you can maintain your confidence for achieving the goal. These are the examples:

- "I am doing well."
- "Let's move forward to my goal."
- "It's definitely alright."
- "Every night comes to an end and morning comes."
- "I decided to do it, and I can do it."

This shake-up period can be quite challenging, as it not only affects your emotions but also physical conditions sometimes. I call this type of shake-up a "comfort zone sickness." For some people, it is so difficult that they want to lower their Gold Vision goals. We must be very mindful not to give in to despair and go back to where we were before setting our goal. As you continue inputting good "imprint type" self-talk messages, it gets calmer. Then, you will be able to see things beyond the current situation.

Another important point for the persevering power is to firmly decide and stick to your decision. What is necessary is to tell your "Subconscious-Me," "I decided to maintain my new comfort zone for achieving my goal."

It is a simple "imprint type" self-talk, but your "Subconscious-Me" receives the message, because it is what you decided to do after all.

Create a Cheering Squad in the Brain That Gives You the Message, "You Can Do It!"

Let me digress a little. Recently, a research study was released on self-talk. Commonly, self-talk messages are expressed in first-person sentences with "I." The research was conducted on the self-talk in the second-person sentence with "you." These second-person messages resulted in high effectiveness as "imprint type" self-talk. (See Figure 5-2.)

Example

"It's alright. I can do it."

"It's alright. You can do it." (Second-person self-talk.)

Which sentence do you feel is more powerful? Especially when you say it aloud, you would agree that the "you" version is quite powerful. When both are compared, you might want to respond: "That's right!" or "Right on," more to the latter expression.

This "you, second-person" self-talk was advocated by Drs. Sandra Dolcos and Dolores Albarracin from the University of Illinois.

In their 2014 paper in the European Journal of Social Psychology titled: "*The inner speech of behavioral regulation: Intentions and task performance strengthen when you talk to yourself as a You.*" It was revealed that task performance was enhanced more when you talk to yourself as "You" than "I."

Those readers who may not click with "you" self-talk might understand it better by imagining having a cheering squad in your brain. After hearing this, an acquaintance of mine commented, "Is it like Shuzo Matsuoka[8], Mr. Positive, in your brain?" Maybe it is easier to get the picture of having someone like him in the brain passionately telling you, "You can do it!"

This "you" self-talk has good compatibility with the concept of the "Subconscious-Me" explained in this book. You talk to your "Subconscious-Me," "You can do it!" Of course, your "Subconscious-Me" is a part of you. Naturally, the "you" self-talk initiated by you comes around and gets back to you. The "you" self-talk offers you such kinds of words.

---

8 Shuzo Matsuoka is a famous Japanese professional tennis player who is known and popular for his passionate and positive character.

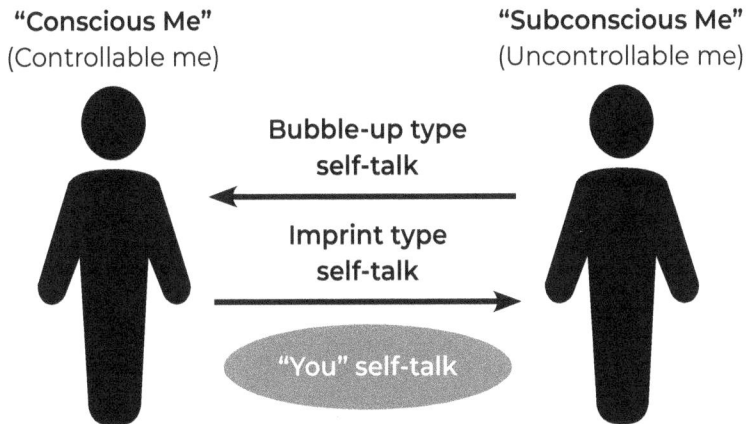

1. Bubble-up type self-talk messages are communicated from "Subconscious Me" to "Conscious Me."
2. Imprint type self-talk messages are communicated from "Conscious Me" to "Subconscious Me."
3. "You" self-talk messages are the imprint type self-talk messages that enhance their effects by beginning the sentence with "you."

Figure 5-2: Self-Talk Mechanism

Confidence Does Not Need the Base

As discussed in Chapter 4, the goal is the future that you create. As we are dealing with the future, your confidence of "you can do it," does not need to have supporting reasons for why you think so. I usually think that "confidence without reasons" is a contradictory expression. However, I also believe that "confidence" in the future naturally does not need reasons.

When you propose something at work, you would be asked to "show the data," which means to "show why you think the proposal can be achieved." However, the data is merely the accumulation of past information. When we talk about the goal of the future, why do we need the past information?

As I repeatedly mentioned, the past is irrelevant to the future. The future creates the past. Therefore, when we discuss materializing the goal, which belongs to the future, we do not need the reasons which belong to the past. Let me introduce you to a familiar example.

When you make a steak dinner, you would not think that you could make it only after compiling some data about your past abilities. Subconsciously, you believe you could make it and start cooking. In this case, "I make delicious steak dinner" is assumed as the goal.

The reason why you can successfully cook it is nothing other than your sense of "I feel I can." Similarly, the reason why you feel confident to achieve your Gold Vision goal can be simply because "I feel I can."

At the end of this chapter, a space is available for "Let's imagine yourself 10 years from now." (See Figure 5-3.) What is written in that space for "what I want to be 10 years from now" will naturally differ from person to person.

If you already have a very high goal, the things you write down for 10 years later could be milestones on the way to achieve it. So, you do not have to stick to the time frame of 10 years, and you might want to change it to 30 years or 40 years from now.

However, everyone should respond in the same way for the columns of "Do you think you can materialize it?" and

"Why do you think so?" Those who have read this book so far would agree.

Your answer will be "*Yes*" for the column, "Do you think you can materialize it?" And your answer will be "*Because I think so*" for the column, "Why do you think so?"

"*Because I think so*" represents the highly efficacious self-talk.

Summary

- "The power to believe in yourself" is the power to firmly believe "I can do it."
- Confidence without reasons is fine as long as you have a clear goal. It differs from those who have high self-evaluation alone.
- Create new circuits in the brain through imprint-type self-talks

Yourself 10 Years From Now	Do you think you can materialize it?	Why do you think so?"

Figure 5-3: Imagine yourself 10 years from now.

CHAPTER 6

Dramatically Attract Gold Vision

The Third Power:
The Power to Involve and Move People

**Why People Always Become Hooked on the Next Trendy
Self-Development Seminar or Program**

The third power is the power necessary for you to strongly attract your Gold Vision into your life.

Sometime after I started coaching, I noticed something peculiar. There were many people who seemed unable to change, even though they set high goals and fully understood the powers to "see the future" and to "believe in yourself."

Why are there some people who can change and some who just cannot, despite their earnest efforts to learn how to do the right things? I thought about it and came to realize that those who could not change have a missing element in common. Let me explain.

Those who manage to successfully change commonly take actions in the spirit of "let's try and see how it goes."

On the other hand, I observed those who couldn't change generally are the character type who want to study everything from the manual before taking an action. They seem afraid of mistakes and failures.

To compensate for this lack of "try and see" attitude, they enthusiastically attend self-development seminars and read hundreds of self-help books.

One would think that after this much study, they would be clear on what to do, but they continue going to seminars and buying more books. They get stuck in the feeling that they don't have enough and need to study more. No matter how many seminars they go to and how many books they read, they cannot get out of their current status quo. They seem to be lost in seminars and self-development books.

One of the reasons these people get stuck, I believe, is that these self-development seminars and books mainly focus on providing knowledge on the systems for change but do not fully show the best ways to take action, how to act.

Perhaps the seminar leaders think that since they taught

the right material in their respective systems, the course participants should be able to follow through on their own and realize their professional or personal goals. Maybe the teachers think it too difficult to really teach people how to move their lives to a new level. Or maybe they themselves do not have enough understandings to be able to teach and lead others to take effective action in their lives.

In any case, those who end up becoming lost in seminars and self-development books, must have started by wanting to change themselves in the first place. This led them to become interested in self-development. It is regrettable that even though they might have enough knowledge, they cannot take a step outside of the status quo - the current version of themselves.

Therefore, I would like to present here my Gold Vision methods regarding how to act if we really want to achieve our goals. This is the unique point of this book, which is not covered in other books.

Since my 20's, I have learned success principles all over the world and I have struggled to apply them in my own life.

Eventually I started multiple companies as an entrepreneur. Thus, I feel proud that I was able to come up with the Gold Vision methodology through the hardships I experienced.

It is certainly a new challenge for me to have readers act by just reading one of my books, without directly working with me as their coach. This book represents my efforts to communicate with readers *when and how to take effective actions* to realize their goals.

My feeling is that more than 90% of people who understand the theories still cannot change. Therefore, this chapter presents the keys for materializing your Gold Vision.

The Brain Knows When to Act

The first key question is when to take an action. Timing is all important. This is true in sports, in cooking, in medicine, in music, and in virtually all other fields. So long as you have established the two pillars for achieving Gold Vision, setting goals and the power to believe in yourself, you will know the appropriate timing for taking actions because of the RAS (Reticular Activating System). Let's review what has been covered in this book thus far:

- The brain cannot hold simultaneously two different comfort zones.
- You set a high goal and strengthen the reality of your comfort zone in the world of your goal. When it truly becomes your new comfort zone, the brain will full-heartedly move toward the higher reality of the goal world and away from the previous comfort zone.
- The RAS, a function of the brain, has the characteristic to filter and allow in only the important information supportive of the goal. Therefore, once you set a goal, the brain selectively recognizes and collects the necessary information for achieving your goal.
- Self-talk comes in two types: bubble-up and imprinting. Create favorable thinking habits with the imprint-type

self-talk, so that your "Subconscious-Me" is filled with positive bubble-up type self-talk, which supports moving toward the new goal. By engaging in this type of self-talk, you can expect to generate great power for reaching your Gold Vision goals.

When a goal is set properly, the necessary information for achieving it comes through the RAS. The brain will let you know when to act. There may be, for some reason, a time when you miss the ideal timing for a given action.

Even in such a case, you don't have to lament that you missed the decisive opportunity. If the goal is set right, another chance will come. Therefore, you can use the imprint-type self-talk, such as: "It's alright to wait for the next chance," or "Let it happen for me again soon." So, don't worry if an opportunity is missed; just take your time and wait for the next chance. It will all work out.

The Comfort Zone is Made Up of People

When the brain lets you know the time to act, you need to be able to do so. Well then, how should we act?

One thing we need to be clear on is what a comfort zone actually consists of. The comfort zone is not about our possessions we own or the money in our bank account. We are not defined by things or money.

For example, let's suppose that you are suddenly gifted a luxury car. Even with this surprising gift, your comfort zone won't change to that of owning a luxury car.

Your comfort zone will stay as it was before; the only difference is the car you drive has changed. You would probably feel somewhat uncomfortable if the only change you have is a luxury car. The same would be true if the change were a gift of an expensive brand-name bag or of winning a million-dollar lottery.

However, if you start interacting with people who own a similar luxury car, your comfort zone will suddenly move. Why is this the case?

The biggest factor that forms a comfort zone, I believe, is people. To move from your current comfort zone to the world of your goal, you need to meet and interact with the people who are already in that new world. With their help, you need to set roots there.

As I mentioned earlier, if you want to leave your present job and start your own company, you need to get out of the circle of people with whom you relate in your current company where you work.

What you need is to actively gather with and interact with entrepreneurs who already live in the world of your goal. Unless you interact with the people who are living in the world of your goal, your comfort zone simply won't change. It is almost as if your current status quo has a gravitational pull.

Some readers might be upset with what I have just written, saying: "Are we supposed to drop and deny our relationships with our current circle of friends and colleagues?" I say 50% yes, 50% no.

If you are to become a resident in the world of your goal, you will need to put more weight on meeting with the people who are in that world; you need to spend more time with them. In this vein, it is true that you will of necessity spend less time with your current and past circle. Thus, the answer is "yes."

However, the reason I say 50% "no" is for example when you graduate from university and become a working adult. Naturally, you no longer see daily the people you used to hang out with as a student, and instead you start developing new relationships in your workplace. This does not mean, though, that you totally cut off the relationships you developed during your school days.

When you set out to move towards your Gold Vision and to change yourself, it is as if you are stepping into a new stage of your life. When the stage you are in changes in this manner, you simply need to meet the people in the new world of your goal.

But please be clear, I am in no way saying that you should change your comfort zone (or people you associate with) according to a sort of profit-loss calculus.

Importance of Sharing a Real Space

In forming a new comfort zone, it is important to be in the same space with the people who belong there already. To communicate with people whom you have never met, it goes much better when we can actually meet in person and talk to them, versus suddenly calling or emailing them. In this way, we can better understand what they want to say.

When we share a space with someone, each other's "Subconscious-Me" is actively in communication. When the subconsciousness is in operation, we get feelings even before we talk, e.g., "I may get along well with that person," or "That person seems to be hard to deal with."

In fact, one's "Subconscious-Me" is influenced by the "Subconscious-Me" of the others who share the space. This is related to homeostasis, an innate property of human nature.

Homeostasis is the function by which humans and animals maintain healthy conditions or functions, such as body temperature, within certain limits for their survival. The comfort zone that we have been discussing in this book operates in this way with regard to homeostasis.

It is understood that the comfort zone applies not only to an individual's physical body but is also shared among the people who share the same space, even beyond the boundary of their physical bodies. Thus, non-verbal communication takes place naturally among their respective "Subconscious-Mes."

It is also understood that in the interaction among the group of "Subconscious-Mes," the ones that maintain a higher level of reality in the comfort zone influence the others. Therefore, when you are in shared space with the people who are in the world of your goal (those who feel so natural to be there), your "Subconscious-Me" receives their positive influences, (the sense of reality in the world of your goal).

In recent years, the quantity of virtual communications through the internet is growing higher, but real face-to-face communication, rather than virtual, is absolutely essential for forming the comfort zone.

Even if it is only once you have shared space with others who have a similar Gold Vision, the sense of reality the group feels will be higher in the subsequent virtual communications.

I used to work for an overseas company stationed in Japan, and most of the meetings were conducted with a video conference system. I found that I could understand those whom I had met, even only once, many times better than those whom I had never met in person.

"The Power to Involve and Move People" Makes a Big Difference

Even when equipped with the same knowledge, there are people who can change and those who can't. What sets them apart is if they can take appropriate action when needed. To break through the status quo, the last critical issue we need to discuss is the power to involve and move people.

The reason I use the expression, "involve and move people," is because I firmly believe that you need many supporters who genuinely believe in you when you work toward your goal. I would say that you will need seven to ten people, if possible, who full-heartedly support you and your efforts and another 20-30 people around them as serious supporters who can more loosely help you.

These numbers are all based on my feelings and experiences, I can say that you can expect a firm support system when you have about seven enthusiastic supporters. Generally, those supporters themselves are busy; therefore, if the number of supporters is just four or five, a shortage of support can result. When the number of supporters is seven, there usually is someone available if a need should arise.

There is a phrase in Japanese, "magical seven." It may be because we generally can deeply relate to about seven people. It is desirable to have three times more people around the core people who can support you in a slightly looser fashion. It is often the case that some of the core people leave when they become busy and need to be replaced. For these circumstances, you would need some candidates who can become core supporters.

These numbers are not exact, but the point that I would like to highlight is the fact that you definitely need people who can cooperate with you when you want to accomplish something big. It is my belief that to materialize your Gold Vision, it is important to consciously ask for help from others in order to generate abundant energy.

When your goal is shared with many people, a great power is generated for strongly supporting the realization of the goal. In fact, those who take actions saying, "let's try it anyway," seem to have intuitively and instinctively this power to involve and move people. Don't worry even if you think of yourself as shy. "The power to involve and move people" is a skill that you can learn and use just like many other things. More specifically, there are seven subsets of power necessary for the power to involve and move people.

1. The power to encounter
2. The power to connect
3. The power to be trusted
4. The power to be recommended
5. The power to communicate
6. The power to implant
7. The power to nurture

Roughly speaking, Items 1 to 4 are the power to be supported by gaining trust, and Items 5-7 are the power to bring others into resonance with your Gold Vision. The relationship between the two groups of items is that the power of Items 1-4 forms the foundation on which implementation takes place using the power of Items 5-7. Now, I would like to explain the 7 subsets of this power listed above.

1. "The Power to Encounter" — Taking the First Step

The first power pertains to encountering people who are living in the world of the goal you are aiming for. How to meet them is simple. You set a goal. When your brain recognizes the goal as your new comfort zone, your "Subconscious-Me" informs you where you should go.

Some hobby examples may give you an easier understanding. When you try to pick up a new hobby, the first step is to go to a gathering of the people who are already doing it. Whether it is running a marathon, scuba diving, or learning how to dance, you would join a circle where you learn and slowly improve your skills. As you improve "your new self who runs marathons," "your new self who scuba dives," or "your new self who dances," the comfort zone of your Gold Vision becomes your new status quo.

The power to encounter is also called for in college graduates' job searching activities. In preparation for going into the world, they would visit prospective workplaces, listen to alumni, and experience internships. As they do so, their comfort zone of being out in the world develops naturally.

The higher your goal is, the higher the hurdle may seem to be "to go and see the residents in the world of the goal." However, many people do it naturally. Don't you feel it less intimidating knowing it is a common practice that many before you have mastered?

When you want to see someone, let's do so full-heartedly, without shying away feeling unequal to the task. You must be careful; what is important here is that seeing someone before setting your goal can have a negative effect.

Let's think of the situation like the following: Realizing the importance of networking with people, a young employee starts exchanging business cards. Normally, they will exchange cards with those in their current comfort zone.

The purpose of the power to encounter is to get an opportunity to move up to the world of your goal. We set the goal and feel the reality of the goal world by meeting with the people who are already there. If your goal is not set, you would end up collecting business cards of the people in your current comfort zone.

Let's suppose that you collected 100 business cards from these people who are in your current status quo. If you are not careful, they might further bind you to this status quo.

Imagine that you are writing thank-you emails to each owner of these 100 business cards or talking to them on the phone or in the online meeting. You will be busy at your current comfort zone and lock yourself in there. In this way, you fail to move toward your goal.

2. "The Power to Connect" — Helping us Stay in the World of the Goal

Of course, just meeting with someone is not good enough. Let's suppose you got a chance to encounter someone you have really wanted to meet. You just had a chat with this person and exchanged business cards and felt excited about getting the opportunity to meet with such an important person. If this is how you approach it, the encounter is likely to be just a one-time event.

To get connected with important people, you need to create a relationship with them beyond just a chat and business-card exchanges.

If you recall the earlier example of hobbies, you, as a total newcomer who does not know much at all, cannot become a part of this new circle without putting in sincere effort to build and sustain relationships.

When you change your job or you are transferred to a new department, you would try to make yourself understood and settle in the new location by taking the initiative to approach people around you and converse with them.

In other words, it is as if you are standing on tiptoes when you have just stepped into the world of your goal. You are not yet stable and grounded in this new world of your Gold Vision. To firmly make the world your new comfort zone and to become a permanent resident there, you need to somehow make contributions to the world.

Unless the newcomers have the intention to contribute, they are usually not accepted particularly well. Nevertheless, the newcomers are standing on tiptoes, and they may be unclear about how they can contribute to their new world.

Perseverance is required here. If you have the intention to contribute, you are likely to find some ways to do so. One effective way is to introduce someone else to the people in the world of the goal.

The comfort zone is made up of people; thus, people are the strongest force for the power to connect.

I understand that this act of introducing someone to others can be challenging, but those who actually do this become successful residents in the world of the goal. I encourage you to use phrases, such as "I have someone in mind who I think you should meet," and "I would like to introduce you to someone." No one would mind being told, "I know someone very interesting, and I would like to introduce you to them."

In the beginning example of this section, we talked about that you met someone with whom you had wanted to connect. Here we can add that you may want to say when you make the exchange, "Well, I have someone I definitely want to introduce you to." You may feel nervous to make this offer to an important person you have just met; you may feel the need of courage to take another step forward.

However, all this discussion is meaningless unless you follow through at that moment. The attitude of "maybe later" would cause you to hesitate or to put this offer off to some future date. It is possible that in the future this important person would not remember meeting you.

You may be wondering if you should introduce yourself first to be understood. While I understand the sentiment, the actuality is that the people in the goal world know that you are a visitor who does not belong to their world.

A harsh reality is that they are evaluating whether or not to accept you in their world. Thus, introducing yourself at this stage could work against you by giving them the impression that you might be trying to sell yourself to them. In this vein, what you need to focus on is simply to generate their general attention to you. Once they start becoming interested in you, they will ask about you.

It is usually desirable to introduce someone who is higher in rank than you are, such as an executive of your client company, an executive of your company, or an experienced senior person. When you introduce your friend or acquaintance whom you respect to someone new, both parties will be pleased.

Even with a person you met for the first time, you might want to say, "While listening to you, I thought of a person I really want to connect you with. The person's name is so and so, and they do such and such. She is a very nice person." Often, the individual will say, "Is that so? Thank you. Please have that person contact me at this email address on my business card."

3. Without "The Power to be Trusted," it is Hard to Be Listened To

Once you get settled in the world of your goal with the power to connect, it is necessary to spread your roots deeply. For that, you need the power to be trusted. The key to this power is the power to believe in yourself, as discussed in Chapter 5.

When you are in the world of the goal on your tiptoes, you are like many people who tend to say, "I am not good enough, but..." or "I am out of place, but..." However, these are taboo phrases.

When you make self-deprecating statements like these, it will be hard to be considered a trustworthy person. Moreover, others might be suspicious of what an out-of-place person is up to, and they might feel that you want to take advantage of them.

On the other hand, they tend to listen carefully to those who speak with full confidence. When someone says, "This is something I definitely recommend," our "Subconscious-Me" is sensitively aware if that person truly means that or not.

Perhaps, you've had experience before when someone recommended something to you, saying, "This is really good." Maybe they were talking about a new movie, or a book, or new music. When the person making the recommendation truly feels the movie (or book or new song) is great, the feeling transmits naturally to you. You would feel inclined to try their recommendation, thinking it must be as good as they say.

This kind of energy is generated more when you are with the people who are moving with a real sense of purpose and energy toward their goals.

People who make self-deprecating comments and seem to look down on themselves do not generate this kind of energy and do not thus pull people into help them reach their goals. People are naturally attracted to the people whose eyes are shining and speaking passionately about what they want to do and about the goals they've developed.

Let's refine your "Subconscious-Me" until you feel 100% confident about what you do and what you say. When your "Subconscious-Me" is enhanced to the level of completely believing in what you say to yourself without any doubt, other people will pick up on your positive attitude.

By strengthening your sense of self-efficacy to the utmost for realizing your goal, your power to be trusted will greatly be enhanced as well to the utmost.

When people respond to your statements and say to you, "Since you recommend such and such, it must be good." It reflects their trust in you. To create these kinds of responses from others, you need to build up your power to believe in yourself.

4. "The Power to be Recommended" Needs a One-Word "Tag" or a Short Phrase to Describe You

When you start hearing from others, "If you recommend such and such, it must be good," you are spreading your roots almost completely in the world of your goal.

When you have just put your toe in to test the waters, you were on the sidelines, so to speak, introducing someone to the people in the world of your goal so as to spread your roots there. That is not yet really being in the world of your goal.

However, you are now at the stage where people will want to introduce you to someone else. This will lead you to the next stage where you can reach higher. To make it simple for someone to recommend you to someone else, you need a one-word "tag" or a short phrase that depicts you succinctly and describes what kind of person you are.

This description is meaningless if it is trite or overblown somehow. Rather you want a description that reflects a true image of you and the person you really want to be—in other words, who you want to be when your goal is achieved. It may not reflect you yet, but you will be able to find the appropriate tag that depicts who you want to be rather easily if you have a clear goal.

One of my clients used to present his business card from the company he was with at that point in time. This was his habit when he socialized with the people in the world of his goal he had set. His business card was quite impressive, because it showed his management title in a prestigious company that everyone knew.

When he started to really grow his roots in the comfort zone of his goal world, he felt more and more that his business card could not be the tag conveying the new image he was building, and so he created a new business card.

The new card reflected the business he was just starting and the one in which he was betting everything he had. When he started exchanging his new business card and started presenting what he really wanted to do with the people in the new world, he felt himself becoming a genuine resident in the world of his goal. He began developing new personal connections that were supportive of his activities.

When someone introduces you to others, what does your tag sound like? You will find your answer easily by looking closely at your goal.

5. "The Power to Communicate" Means Communications Among the "Subconscious-Mes"

From this section on, the focus will be on the powers necessary to bring others into resonance with your Gold Vision. For that purpose, you need what your Gold Vision is to be properly understood. However, if you start talking about your Gold Vision right away after you have just stepped into the comfort zone of the new goal world, people in that world might be understandably a bit apprehensive about what you are saying.

You will be like a newcomer to them with no track record at all, starting to talk passionately about some big project. No matter how wonderful your goal might sound, no one will likely listen to it and embrace it right away. Therefore, the important groundwork for you to work on is to establish supportive human relations in the world of your goal, as discussed in Items 1-4 above.

For example, if someone asks you, "By the way, what work do you do?" This is a perfect opportunity for you to talk about your Gold Vision. Perhaps, the person will say, "Really? Why didn't you tell me sooner?" It is desirable in other words for you to wait for the right timing when someone does ask you about your goals and vision. When that happens, how effectively do you communicate about your Gold Vision?

At the beginning of this chapter, I mentioned that effective communication is dependent on the mutual messaging at the level of your respective "Subconscious-Me." Without speaking, non-verbal communication takes place naturally between your "Subconscious-Me" and the other's "Subconscious-Me."

In other words, when your "Subconscious-Me" strongly believes in the comfort zone in the world of your goal, your Gold Vision is communicated naturally to the other's "Subconscious-Me." When you propose something, the other might say "that's great," or reject it. In a way, the other's "Subconscious-Me" has already decided beforehand.

When these factors are understood well, your approach to communication itself may change. Those who are listening to you will be more aware of what kind of person you are at their subconscious level than through what you actually say.

It is important of course to polish the contents of what you want to convey; however, you would understand what is far more important in this situation is to hone your "power to see the future" and your "power to believe in yourself."

6. Successful Salespeople Have a Good Command of "The Power to Implant"

As has been discussed that major communication takes place at the deeper level of the "Subconscious-Me," the actual verbal communication that follows is simply to confirm what the "Subconscious-Me" already knows.

As the contents of the communications at the level of "Subconscious-Me" do not come up to the conscious level, verbal communications play an important role in helping the listener understand them consciously. In particular, it is important not to force one's opinions on anyone else.

When people feel they are being forced to a certain point of view, their "Subconscious-Me" naturally rebels against this effort, no matter how good the thoughts might be.

As discussed already many times in this book, humans' instincts will always strive to maintain the status quo. Therefore, the "Subconscious-Me" tries to eliminate all sorts of influences that bring changes to the status quo and will end up rebelling against the new information.

In this sense, I disagree with the argument that it is better to make a complete presentation of your Gold Vision all at once. A full, smooth presentation might sound agreeable while listening, but it is often forgotten when it is finished. This is because listening like this takes place at the conscious level and will not reach into the subconscious level.

It is desirable therefore to intentionally break up the information into smaller elements and create some empty space between presenting them. Then, the listener's "Subconscious-Me" spontaneously organizes the information based on what they've just heard and fills in the gaps.

As a result, the contents of the presentation are thought of as if they were one's own ideas.

Thus, we can let nature take her course, so that the listener's "Subconscious-Me" becomes self-convinced. Letting nature take her course, however, does not mean leaving things completely up to nature by doing nothing.

It is important for us to implant the necessary information little by little, and in this way helping the listener's "Subconscious-Me" understand our Gold Vision. My feeling is that the best amount of information is the level where the listener says, "Please let me hear more about it." Then the next step is to wait until the implanted information grows in the listener's "Subconscious-Me."

In fact, good salespeople have a good command of this "power to implant." They do not speak about the merits of the products they want to sell all at once, but they selectively provide the information in small batches according to the other person's interest.

The key phrase many salespeople say is something like, "Please excuse me now, as I have to go to another appointment." In that way they limit the information they have shared to a small and digestible amount.

They regularly visit the client and increase the information they're providing to the "Subconscious-Me" in stages. The client's mind gradually comes to the point of thinking, "Maybe I should try this new product (or new service)." Eventually, the client starts to feel, "I want this product because I need it."

In truth, the salesperson's implanting power was behind it all, but the client never recognized it. They don't think, "I'm buying this because the salesperson recommended it to me." Rather, they, like most other humans, tend to believe they arrived at their decision on their own.

Let's think of this case in the context of Gold Vision. You don't have to press your message hard on others. You don't have to say, "Please help me achieve my Gold Vision." What you want to create is a situation in which the others would naturally support you.

It is not the case that all salespeople have a good command of this "power to implant." It is like a secret skill that successful salespeople naturally use. They are those who firmly believe that their products will definitely help their clients and thus are motivated to generate the sale. In the same manner, when you sincerely believe in your Gold Vision, it won't be so difficult for you to make use of this "power to implant."

So, let's find our own way of "the power to implant" by remembering two key points: Don't force your Gold Vision on anyone, but offer the information in small, digestible pieces.

7. Without "The Power to Nurture," Flowers Do Not Bloom

Even if we put our efforts into sowing seeds and planting seedlings, the young plants will die if they are neglected. To produce flowers and fruits, the important thing is to assist them to grow by watering and fertilizing them. Sometimes they need to be moved to get more sun.

"The Power to Nurture" is indispensable if you want to have big-bloomed flowers resulting from your efforts.

Similarly, the information you communicated to the other person's "Subconscious-Me" with your "power to implant" must be carefully nurtured.

It is hard to recall the face of the person with whom you had a chat and received a business card six months ago. Unless you from time to time remind the people you met and gave cards to, they will forget your existence easily.

- Talk to them face to face.
- Call them.
- Write a letter.
- Send an email.

There are many ways to remind them. The use of social media is also effective, as you can quite casually remind them.

This is a similar job to laying groundwork for passing through your business plan. Usually, it is unlikely that your business plan will be accepted the first time that you present it. You need to continue to present your business plan as you update and talk about it with many people, including key players. At some point, someone will remember it saying, "Oh, that's what s/he was talking about. Maybe we should have him/her try it."

Similarly, as you continue reminding others around you of your Gold Vision, people around you naturally start supporting you to achieve your goals, saying, "Shall I introduce you to someone who knows about what you are intending to do?" or "I have such and such information."

If you feel that you do a lot of things, but you feel nothing is growing, it means that your way of doing things may need to be improved. It only means that you need to devise a better way or find other ways.

The power to involve and move people, which consists of seven sub-powers, was discussed and is the last decisive "power" to give you a supportive push forward for achieving your Gold Vision. All these powers really become forceful when they start functioning naturally at the level of your "Subconscious-Me."

For that purpose, as mentioned repeatedly in this book, two pillars of Gold Vision Method must be firmly built— setting a high goal and the power to believe in yourself. These two factors are deeply related to all of the other factors. Thus, these two pillars are most important, as we cannot expect anything to happen without them.

You have already learned various things about three powers that are required for breakthrough. The only thing left now is to practice them. Set a goal outside of the status quo. With favorable imprint-type self-talks, fill "Subconscious-Me" up with "the power to believe in yourself."

You now know how to do them. To change yourself now and jump into the new world, let's take the first step.

Summary

- "The power to involve and move people" means the power to have other people's trust and support. They will then resonate with your Gold Vision.
- The comfort zone is made up of people.
- Strengthening the power to involve and move people requires 7 sub-powers.

CLOSING

Life Changes With Gold Vision

My Life Changed With Gold Vision

U p to this point, I have mentioned the method to transcend and break through the status quo with Gold Vision by introducing various examples. As mentioned in the Introduction, all my clients who I coached using the Gold Vision Method were able to break away from the fear that they had had about themselves and succeeded in flying into the world of their goals.

The door to Gold Vision is opened equally in front of everybody.

I am also one of those who were able to greatly change their life using Gold Vision. Previously, my life had been filled with many failures as well as trials and errors. Thus, I am whole-heartedly convinced about the value of Gold Vision and sincerely hope that many people will make use of it.

In this vein, I want to introduce my personal experiences for the readers' reference.

Because of my father's work, I lived in San Francisco from when I was one-year old to six-years old. Living in the United States during my childhood had a significant influence on my life later on.

In the United States, you are expected to speak out and asserting yourself is considered a commendable act. Also, the bigger your dreams are, the better. At least, I felt that way. In my early childhood, my dream was to become the President of the United States of America.

My goal was indeed set far beyond the status quo. The time was the 1970s, and it was still not so rare for Asians to be discriminated against. As a child, I was wondering and feeling resentment about that. So, I purely wanted to become the most influential person in the world and change the world for the better.

Since My Childhood, "Helping Others" Was My Interest

As I grew up in the environment of American values, I had a hard time adjusting after returning to Japan.

Above all, it was so difficult to get the feeling of Confucian teaching regarding the relationship between senior and junior. My Japanese classmates naturally had been ingrained in that feeling, but I hadn't.

In the US several times I heard some friends call their mother by her first name. (Rather than calling her "Mom," or "Mother," they would call, for example, "Susan.") I don't know whether that was common, but my impression was that in the main parents and children were equal, and basically so were teachers and students.

From what I saw, what parents said was enforceable in US, of course, children often were deemed worthy of respect in the same way as adults were. Due to this type of American upbringing, I must have appeared reckless, impolite, and sometimes rude to my teachers in my Japanese school after having come back from US.

Reading the situation was very difficult for me. Of course, people were sensitive to the mood in the US as well. However, when something must be expressed, they seemed to give it a priority. In Japan, on the other hand, it is not necessarily so. I have experienced many situations in Japan in which everyone just remains quiet, believing it is "better not to say anything."

In these circumstances, my behavior where I was daring to speak out what I believed was right must have been annoying for the people around me. It was not so obvious in the lower grades of primary school, but people around me started giving me a cold look for not reading the situations as I got older.

For example, when the class was going to decide on our

class representative, I would cheerfully raise my hand to be a candidate, as I liked to appear in front of people and was a leader type of person. However, there were a few times that my classmates would say, "It is better to have someone else, other than Hisano-san," and didn't want to make me the representative.

It was somewhat like bullying. I felt uncomfortable, but I did not change my style, as I did not understand why it was bothering the other children. Ordinarily, they would have bullied me more saying, "cheeky monkey."

One of the reasons why they didn't was maybe because I did well in school. Before tests, some classmates would come to me asking for help or if we could study together. I taught them sincerely; therefore, they must have thought about me being a naughty, but still mostly a good, guy.

Besides, liking to appear in front of people and being a leader type, I had another characteristic which was that I loved being useful to others. When someone asked me to teach, I was so happy to be helpful. I often ended up teaching for two hours, in spite of the initial plan of 20 minutes.

As those friends I taught started understanding what they didn't get before, I got more energized. In front of my eyes, their scores were getting better. Naturally, my motivation to teach was further enhanced.

I started realizing, "My hobby is to help others." As I read history cartoon books, I was getting the brass to imagine such big dreams as, "If I were an emperor, I could make the world better."

By then, I knew my nationality did not allow me to become President of the United States of America. So, my next dream was to become Prime Minister of Japan. Without any basis, I somehow felt, "I must be able to do it." In retrospect, I was already practicing "confidence without grounds."

Selecting a Path to Become a Statesman

As I became a teenager, I, who had great confidence, came to realize that it was not so easy to become a statesman, because I was born in the family of a corporate employee with no connection to politics. So, I thought hard about how I could materialize my dream.

The practical paths seemed to be becoming a secretary for a politician, inheriting the electoral turf by possibly marrying a politician's daughter, and working as a bureaucrat and then becoming a politician after retirement.

To jump into the political world from no base, generally these are the possible paths to follow, but nothing really appealed to me. So, I thought I would walk a different path from the other candidates for political office.

Around that time, I was touched by reading Dale Carnegie's *How to Win Friends and Influence People*, which I happened to find on my father's bookshelf. Since then, I have read many self-help books. Thanks to these books, I feel my backbone of how I wanted to live my life developed. That was to "decide your life on your own."

Due to my father's work, my family moved again to

London, when I was a freshman in high school, and I started as a vocalist for a rock band.

Back then, hard rock was very popular, the band was looking for a singer who had a high-tone voice, and I was singled out. As I was enthusiastically working at it, I thought that it might be good to be famous with the band, and then run for election.

Initially, I looked at my music as a step for becoming a politician, but it was surprisingly enjoyable in itself. My passion for politics cooled down, and inversely my passion for music grew increasingly. I decided to "Shoot for the world with music!"

After I continued my education into university, my passion for music did not calm down. Instead of attending classes, I was often enthusiastically engaged in the band's activities.

One day when I was 20 years old, the owner of the vocal school where I was going asked me out of the blue, "Hisano-san, I want to ask you something. Don't you want to teach here?"

As a young man, I was surprised by the offer; nevertheless, I started teaching there. This was a great turning point in my life.

A Business Owner in My 20's With No Boss

Besides my dream to become a politician, since I was young, I also thought that I would like to start my own business someday.

My father worked for a salary, but for his children his attitude was "It is not mandatory to go to high school or university and to join a company like many people commonly do. Choose your own path where you can make a contribution." Thus, I was not assuming I would get a job fresh out of university.

In this environment, I put my efforts mostly into my band activities and teaching at the vocal school. I ended up failing to get all of the necessary credits and had to stay at the university one extra year.

When I graduated, I did not seek a regular job, but started my own business right away. One of the reasons was that it seemed difficult for me to do well in a traditional office setting, as I was still not fitting in totally in the Confucian teaching regarding the relationship between senior and junior.

The first business I started after graduating from the university was a vocal school utilizing my experience so far. Besides having accumulated enough experience, I had always liked teaching others since I was a child. I felt this business quite suitable for me.

Later when I was 27 years old, I started a mail order company and transitioned quite smoothly into being a businessman. However, I was gradually getting anxious and uncertain if I should continue in that direction.

Though I continued music after graduating from the university, I already knew that I didn't have the talent to aim for true success as a world musician.

I started to ask myself, "what do I want to become?"

If I continued my businesses, I might remain a business owner earning reasonably well, but I might end up just that.

As I started a business on my own, I had no boss and no senior who could teach me about the business world and its ways.

Realizing something was missing in me, I started attending various self-help seminars and reading numerous business books so as to grow as a businessman and also to relieve my anxiety. However, I had difficulty finding clear answers.

When I reached the milestone age of 30-years old, my feeling that I could not stay as I had been began to grow further.

"How can I become a better businessman?" became an important quest and question for me.

My answer was to get a job at a corporation.

Top Sales Record in Six Months After Joining the Company

As I started my own business right after graduating from the university, I did not know about companies in the world in general. I thought that by learning about the organization of a company, I would be able to gain a broader view as how management worked. Thus, I chose to find employment.

The first company I joined at 30 was a job-placement company that focused on supporting job-placement in the information and advertisement fields. I was employed there as a salesperson.

For the first six months I worked as an employee, I worked desperately hard and became far and away the best salesperson.

I don't mean to brag about it. Rather, I want to share the reasons why it was possible for me, a complete beginner, to achieve such a record. Thus, I want to convey the effects of Gold Vision to the readers.

Soon after having started my job, I noticed big differences in work attitude between the senior employees and myself. The biggest difference was the belief in "can do" attitude.

For example, the company I joined had a big company that they had been working to build a relationship with, but so far unsuccessfully. They had not even been able to schedule an appointment to meet and talk to them.

One day, the president gave me an order saying, "Mr. Hisano, how would you approach them? Try to get an appointment with the company."

The senior employees' looks were telling me, "We have attacked them for many years, but we couldn't get anywhere. No matter what his strategy is, it won't work," or "He is a newcomer. No way he can get in with them."

When I called the company to set up an appointment, their answer was blunt and curt, and I understood how hard it must have been for my seniors. Nevertheless, I tried and tried with my determination to absolutely get an appointment and persistently appealed to them how valuable my company's recruitment advertisements were.

After many twists and turns, I succeeded to get an

appointment with them. In addition to that, they finally gave us a contract (a very big one).

The other thing that I noticed when watching the senior employees was that they were bound by the fixed idea of vertical organization, for example, that the sales department did only sales and the sales planning department did only planning.

I was then transferred to the sales planning department, but I was indifferent to such a vertical way of thinking, and I did everything I could do to continue to make the clients happy.

Back then, my Gold Vision was "a happy client's face." This is what I focused on. By doing so, despite my handicap of being a 30-year-old newcomer, I was able to break through the status quo.

When I had subordinates later, based on these findings, I started sharing my method with them. My subordinates who would not be called "good salespeople" by any standard, ended up achieving remarkable results one after another.

Encountering Coaching

Including the changes in my subordinates, it was amazing to see the effects in business by applying what I learned in many seminars and books. I wanted to learn more, and I continued studying self-development, while still working in the company.

Subsequently, I accumulated experiences by taking on many responsible positions in sales, finance, marketing, corporate planning, logistics, new business start-ups, etc.

in various companies, mostly foreign companies in Japan, with different industry types and cultures.

As a typical office worker, I also had my share of frustrations within the organizations, including demotion. However, I was not discouraged—rather, I worked hard, aiming to come back again. In fact, in the case where I was demoted, I was able to later get a promotion.

Then, encountering a book opened a new door to a different life for me. It was a book that introduced TPIE (Tice Principles in Excellence), which was co-authored by Lou Tice and Dr. Hideto Tomabechi. I read this book and felt "This is it; it's so complete!"

The book clearly answered my questions about the self-help theories that I had studied and had been wondering if they were applicable only to some people. The book struck me as highly important; I felt I was destined to find "the real thing." I signed up right away for a TPIE seminar, which had just landed in Japan.

The more I learned the coaching theories backed up with cognitive science, the deeper I was convinced that this method could surely lead anybody to be successful.

What I learned from TPIE was immediately applicable to my work. Setting proper goals, improving self-talk messages, and understanding comfort zones became new special skills that were added to my management-related job and differentiated me from the other managers.

Of course, I began thinking about my own goals that would go beyond the status quo.

My Gold Vision

Around that time, I was given a big job in my company, of which the sales amounted to tens of billions of dollars. My goal then was to be the CEO of such a world-class company.

With this in mind, I graduated at the top of my class at Tsukuba University's MBA program. It is one of only a few in Japan that requires English in lectures and the master-degree thesis.

Originally, I thought of getting an MBA at an overseas university, but it was difficult to go abroad due to my family situation.

I worked hard indeed with the thought that if I could graduate at the top of my class from a Japanese university, I could in effect bridge the gap between my getting a degree from a top US MBA program and the one I would get from the Japanese university.

Thus, I was moving toward my goal to be the top of a world-class company. According to the TPIE coaching theory, I started my daily imprint-type self-talks such as "I am the CEO of a world-class company" and "I am one of the top managers in the world."

At times when the president was absent, (with the approval of his secretary) I walked into his office and sat in his chair to enhance my sense of reality of being there and viewing what I would see.

Unfortunately, however, my "Subconscious-Me" was not totally convinced by my goal "to be the president of a world-class company" and my imprint-type self-talks that

I came up with. I felt frustration that the energy to move forward to the goal was not sufficiently generated.

When I came to think of it, I realized the goal to be the president of a world-class company was derived from thinking that I had a good chance for the job based on my past experiences, skills, and potentials.

Was it, however, really what I wanted to do wholeheartedly? Was it my wanting-to goal?

When I reconsidered what my heart really wanted to do, my goal surfaced and changed to "become the best in the world with coaching."

Since my childhood, I liked to help others and was good at teaching. I had already been practicing coaching and feeling delighted seeing many people change. Coaching had already been developing as my lifework.

From my university days, I felt it would be difficult to work in a salaried position. Nevertheless, I felt it was necessary for me to experience working in an organization. Since I was 30 years of age, I lived the corporate life and was quite successful. Even so, the longer I continued, the more I felt something wasn't right. Perhaps, it meant that such a job was difficult for me after all. After many trials and errors, I finally found my Gold Vision in my mid-30s.

Wanting to Find "This Way" Together

As Lou Tice's words, "The goal comes first, then the reality follows," I got a pile of new findings every day. I was amazed how much I was constrained by scotomas.

Since I began doing what I wanted to do wholeheartedly, day-to-day activities and my goal were perfectly synchronized and the world that I saw increasingly changed.

This was something that I already had a conscious understanding of, but as I personally experienced it, I was impressed anew.

Currently, I have literally no doubt about materializing my goal. I have arrived at the stage where I can clearly explain what people need for achieving their goals. Honestly, my path to get here was long and steep, but now that I have arrived, I can say it was a wonderful experience.

Because I feel so wonderful, I want to share that feeling with as many people as possible.

Everyone is born with great talents, but there are so many people who do not realize them. However, with Gold Vision, it is possible to continually express and blossom these hidden talents, even those unknown to oneself.

People all over the world can find their own talents, learn how to use their cognitive resources properly, and live a fulfilling and happy life.

Then I believe that society will change, nations will change, and the world will change for the better.

My goal is not the same as what I dreamed as a child, "Becoming the President of the United States of America," but its essence remains unchanged: I am still working to make the world a better place.

The name of my company that I started is Conoway: "Cono" in Japanese means "this" and therefore Conoway means "this way." It is the way for each person to move toward his/her own Gold Vision.

I want to be with those who want to change themselves and go beyond the status quo by finding their own unique version of "This Way."

With such a hope, I wish this book will be in the hands of as many people as possible.

EPILOGUE

Since this book's original Japanese publication in 2016, the world has changed to an astonishing degree during just these six years.

The pandemic caused by COVID-19 alone, of course, has had a huge impact on the world. In addition, wars, political dictatorships, political and social divisions in various places, and conflicts between superpowers are all interrelated, resulting in the world's resource shortages, labor shortages, and soaring prices. These situations are creating economic instability in the world.

Consequently, the gaps between the haves and the have-nots and between the strong and the weak are further widening and leading to conflicts.

From a broader perspective, most would agree that this current situation is not desirable for anyone. However, from an individualistic viewpoint, many people cannot afford to worry about others, as their harsh reality is that all they can do is to take care of themselves and their families first and foremost.

On the other hand, there are movements starting in some parts of the world where people are taking back power into their own hands—power that has long been held by nations and giant corporations and everyone is living his/her own authentic life in the community. Though the wave of such movements may be still small, it is steadily gaining momentum.

Throughout our history, we humans have been tossed around by numerous natural and man-made disasters. Yet, without losing hope, many of us have continued walking forward, even in difficult situations and finding light and hope in our future. The driving force behind this determination has always been our Gold Vision, which is presented in this book. Thanks to those individuals who continued to hold on to their Gold Vision and worked toward its materialization, even in the most desperate situations, we have seen humans thrive and make progress.

Through this book, if I could convey the message that your Gold Vision has such a power to better your life and the lives of the people you care about, I am more than happy. Furthermore, if you feel that you can carry out even greater leadership, please do create a grand vision to make a big impact on the world.

It is my sincere hope that this book will contribute to readers envisioning their own Gold Vision and creating a bright future for themselves and those who are around them.

My heartfelt gratitude goes to Noriko Hosoyamada, president of PCS Inc, for her efforts in translating the original Japanese version into English and publishing this book. Also, I would like to acknowledge Bob Quinn and Beth Simone for their great support in editing the book.

It all began in the beginning of 2020 in the United States, when Noriko came across my online course of Gold Vision University provided in Japanese. She immediately signed up for the course and shared it with her husband, Norman Bodek, then president of PCS. Shortly after, this encounter turned into a project of Norman's to publish *CEO Coaching*, my first book in English, around the end of the year just before his passing. Without their help, the publication of this book, *Gold Vision*, in English would have been much delayed.

My appreciation also goes to each of those who helped me develop the Gold Vision method as it is now. Gold Vision would not have been this successful without the understanding supporters who always challenged me to improve the concept.

Finally, I would like to dedicate this book to my wife, Seiko, whom I deeply love and respect, and my son, Sho, whom I cherish and whose future I look forward to. Because of their existence, I have been able to continuously envision my Gold Vision. I am always thankful for them.

It is a great joy for me to have this book published and become available in English, as it can reach more people than ever and help them learn about Gold Vision.

October 22, 2022, Kazuyoshi Hisano

REFERENCES

Dale Carnegie, *How to Win Friends and Influence People* (*Hito wo Ugokasu*, Japanese translation by Hiroshi Yamaguchi, Sogensha)

Napoleon Hill, *Think and Grow Rich* (*Shikowa Genjitsukasuru*, Japanese translation by Takaaki Tanaka, Kikoshobo)

Mark Fisher, *The Instant Millionaire* (*Seikono Okite*, Japanese translation by Yayoi Uemaki with supervision by Sumio Kondo, JAMM)

Stephen R. Covey, *The Seven Habits of Highly Effective People* (*Nanatsuno Shukan*, Japanese translation by James Skinner and Shigeru Kawanishi, Kingbear Publishing)

Daniel Goldman, *Emotional Intelligence: Why it can matter more than IQ* (*EQ: Kokorono IQ*, Japanese translation by Kyoko Tsuchiya, Kodansha)

Spencer Johnson M.D., *One Minute for Yourself* (*Ippunkan Jikoka-kumei*, Japanese translation by Kaoru Kobayashi, Diamond Inc.)

James C. Collins and Jerry I Porras, *Built to Last: Successful Habits of Visionary Companies*, (*Visionary Company*, Japanese translation by Yoichi Yamaoka, Nikkei BP)

James C. Collins and Jerry I. Porras, *Built to Last: Successful Habits of Visionary Companies (Good to Great Book 2)* (*Visionary Comapny 2*, Japanese translation by Yoichi Yamaoka, Nikkei BP)

Hideto Tomabechi, *Mazuwa Oyawo Koenasai* (Surpass Your Parents First), Forest Publishing

Hideto Tomabechi, *Kokorono Soujyujyutsu* (Mind-Operation Skills), PHP Interface

Hideto Tomabechi, *Ninchi-Kagaku-eno Shotai* (Invitation to Cognitive Science), Cyzo Inc.

Hideto Tomabechi, *Jibunwo Okikukaeru Ijintachi, 100no Kotoba* (Collection of 100 Sayings of Great People), TAC Publishing

Lou Tice, *Smart Talk* (*Affirmation*, Japanese translation by Miwa Taguchi with supervision by Hideto Tomabechi), Forest Publishing

Daniel Coyle, *The Little Book of Talent: 52 Tips for Improving Your Skills* (*Sainowo Nobasu Simplena Hon*, Japanese translation by Takashi Yumiba, Sunmark Publishing)

Marcus Buckingham, *The One Thing You Need to Know About Great Managing, Grate Leading and Sustained Individual Success* (*Saikonomanagerga Itsumokangaeteiru Tattahitotsunokoto*, Japanese translation by Takuro Kagayama, Nikkei Inc.)

Ken Honda, *Yudayajin Fugono Oshie* (The Millionaire's Philosophy for a Happy Life), Daiwashobo

Masanori Kanda, *Hijyoshikina Seikohosoku* (Unorthodox Ways to Achieve Success), Forest Publishing

Kenichiro Okano, *Nokaramieru Kokoro* (The Heart Seen from the Brain), Iwasaki Academic Publisher

Yuji Iketani, *Tanjyunna Nou, Fukuzatsuna "Watashi"* (Simple Brain, Complex "I"), Kokansha

Peter Thiel with Blake Masters, *Zero to One*, (*Zero to One*, Japanese translation by Miwa Seki, NHK Publishing)

John P. Kotter, *Leading Change*, (*Kigyo-Henkakuryoku*, Japanese translation by Hiroyoshi Umezu, Nikkei BP)

Etsuko Okajima, Battekisareruhitono Ningenryoku (Human Strength of Those Who Are Selected), Toyo Keizai Inc.

Hiroyuki Ishii, *Kokorono Brakeno Hazushikata* (How to Release the Mind's Brake), Forest Publishing

Lou Tice with Joyce Quick, *Personal Coaching for Results*, Thomas Nelson Inc.

R. C. Schank, *The Cognitive Computer* (*Kangaeru Computer*, Japanese translation by Shun Ishizaki with supervision by Kazuhiro Fuchi, Diamond Inc.)

INDEX

T

www.ingramcontent.com/pod-product-compliance
Lightning Source LLC
Chambersburg PA
CBHW051521120626
46551CB00012B/1027